John Davis' provocative book goes  dared to write about 'seeing' God. and insightful. They are certain to of your heart that you might see God in ways you may have considered.

BOB RUSSELL
Retired Senior Minister, Southeast Christian Church, Louisville, Kentucky

I do not usually read former students' manuscripts, but this time I'm glad I did. I sincerely appreciate what John has done on this seldom-addressed subject. He found many relevant angles to develop and unfolded them in ways that are very relevant to Christian thinking and living. I believe it will be a great help for all Christians in our pursuit of sanctification—trying to be perfect as God is perfect (Matthew 5:48). I was quite moved many times as I was reading it.

JACK COTTRELL (1938-2022)
Author, Pastor, Teacher

If John Owen is right to say that 'No man shall ever behold the glory of Christ by sight hereafter, who doth not in some measure behold it by faith here in this world,' then every Christian has much invested in that which John Davis attends to in this book. We were made to see the unseen and unseeable God. The paradoxical nature of this claim is no effectual deterrent for the heart that has been awaked by faith to behold the glory of God in the face of Jesus Christ (2 Cor 4:6). Indeed, since worship of the Triune God is positively driven by his mysterious transcendence, the heart that has been awakened by faith delights in the ineffability of Christian truth: Christ has made the invisible God visible—the God whom no one has ever seen nor can see is nevertheless seen with the eyes of faith now and shall be seen in glory in the beatific vision. My affections were stirred while reading Seeing the Unseen God, and I heartily commend it. Not only is it thoroughly biblical, but it is also pastorally sensitive. Read this book and let Pastor Davis shepherd you into the presence of Christ, in whose face you will see the glory of the unseen God.

SAMUEL G. PARKISON
Assistant Professor of Theological Studies,
Gulf Theological Seminary, United Arab Emirates;
Author, *Irresistible Beauty: Beholding the Triune Glory in the Face of Jesus Christ*

Many Christians find difficulty living in the tensions of Scripture, and fewer yet are brave enough to write about it. John Davis has done this and quite well. In his book, *Seeing the Unseen God*, Davis captures the biblical tension of the call to spend our lives as Christians seeking what we cannot see as the path to truly know the Triune God. John Davis is a biblically sound, pastorally sensitive guide for you throughout this important tension and I trust, as you read, you will be in good hands.

BRIAN CROFT
Executive Director, Practical Shepherding

JOHN DAVIS

SEEING
THE UNSEEN
GOD

CHRISTIAN
FOCUS

Copyright © John Davis 2023

paperback ISBN 978-1-5271-1001-4
ebook ISBN 978-1-5271-1055-7

10 9 8 7 6 5 4 3 2 1

Published in 2023
by
Christian Focus Publications Ltd,
Geanies House, Fearn, Ross-shire,
IV20 1TW, Great Britain.

www.christianfocus.com

Cover design by
Rubner Durais

Printed and bound by
Bell & Bain, Glasgow

Contents

Introduction 9

Chapter 1 No one has ever seen God 13

Chapter 2 You cannot see God and live 19

Chapter 3 The second commandment 27

Chapter 4 Seeing God in Jesus Christ 35

Chapter 5 Seeing God in one another 45

Chapter 6 The primary way we see God: The Bible 53

Chapter 7 Beauty, wonder, and moments of transcendence 63

Chapter 8 What happens when you see God? 71

Chapter 9 Spiritual blindness 81

Chapter 10 Seeing God when it seems He is not there 91

Chapter 11 The pure in heart 103

Chapter 12 The light that gives sight 111

Chapter 13 A desire to see God 121

Chapter 14 The gaze of the soul 131

Chapter 15 You must work hard to see God 137

Chapter 16 Looking forward to the reward 145

Chapter 17 God sees us 155

Conclusion Seeing Him who is invisible 163

Scripture Index 167

*To my wife and my best friend, Jennifer,
without whom I wouldn't have
the spirit, confidence, or peace
to write something like this.
The Lord has been so good to us.*

INTRODUCTION

What I am advocating for in this book is impossible. The biblical authors say no one has ever done it. Not only that, they say you can't do it even if you try. Yet at the same time, they will tell you it is absolutely essential. Sounds encouraging, right? It's like that moment in every *Mission Impossible* movie where Ethan Hunt starts explaining the mission to his team, and they all tell him he's out of his mind. To live the Christian life, you *must* do what you *cannot* do.

What we are after in this book is seeing God. In the first few chapters you will learn why this initially seems like an exercise in futility. By the end, however, I hope to have shown you that not only is it possible, it is the most important and rewarding pursuit of your life. You cannot walk the Christian life or find true happiness without it. It is a quest that will frustrate you and confuse you at times. You will never fully achieve success—at least not on this side of eternity. But the constant pursuit of it is what this life is all about.

A Devotional Theology of Seeing God

What comes to mind when you hear the word *theology?* Perhaps an out-of-touch old man in a dress-robe, smoking a pipe, sitting in a leather chair, surrounded by shelves and shelves of books? Professors at universities engaging in debates about topics most of us never even think about? If that's what you think you're not alone, but it's not what you should think and here is why: theology is, simply, the study of God. This is not a pursuit limited merely to the brainiacs nor the elite. Rather, it's the pursuit of an answer to the question, "What can we know about God?". Thus, if we live in a world made by God and ruled by God, there is absolutely nothing more practical and relevant than theology.

Two overarching convictions are shaping every word I write in this book. First, the Bible is where God has revealed who He is; second, all proper theology should lead to worship. This book is a biblical study of the pursuit to see God. And since the Bible is God's own self-revelation to us, we are essentially looking at the instructions God Himself has given us on how to see Him.

But it cannot and must not stop there. It must lead to worship. Boring theology is an absolute tragedy. It shouldn't exist. The phrase *devotional theology* should sound unnecessarily repetitive, like 'wet water' or 'disgusting cauliflower.' Unfortunately, there are hundreds of books out there filled with facts about God and the Bible, yet dry as a bone. I have worked hard not to allow that to happen here. This is not an exhaustive academic work. It is not meant to be used primarily as a reference book. I have tried my best to provide you with theology to fuel your worship—devotional theology.

But, on the other hand, do not think because I say *devotional* that it is in the same category as the fluffy, 'positive and encouraging' books you might be used to seeing on the Christian best-seller lists. I will not hide my disappointment for all the junk that has been served up to the church my entire life. Books that give the people what they want, that feed our egos and self-importance, that *use* the Bible as a way to baptize the author's own worldly wisdom, are far too common and are doing much more harm than good. This is not a book full of my personal musings. This is a biblical study. C. S. Lewis once wrote,

> For my own part I tend to find the doctrinal books often more helpful in devotion than the devotional books, and I rather suspect that the same experience may await many others. I believe that many who find that 'nothing happens' when they sit down, or kneel down, to a book of devotion, would find that the heart sings unbidden while they are working their way through a tough bit of theology with a pipe in their teeth and a pencil in their hand.[1]

---

1. C. S. Lewis, *Introduction to Athanasius' On the Incarnation*, https://www.bhmc.org.uk/uploads/9/1/7/7/91773502/lewis-incarnation-intro.pdf

In my opinion, the very best books make you consistently stop reading to do three things (though not necessarily all at the same time): worship, pray, or write notes in your Bible. It is my hope, my prayer, and my intention that this book would do that for you.

One Thing

David writes in Psalm 27:4, 'One thing have I asked of the Lord, that will I seek after: that I may dwell in the house of the Lord all the days of my life, to gaze upon the beauty of the Lord and to inquire in his temple.'

One thing. This is David's single-minded, undivided, laser-focused pursuit. Nothing else matters compared to gazing upon the beauty of the Lord. Seeing God. This book is my challenge to all of us to be just like David. To pursue seeing God above everything else. We want to be like Moses on Mount Sinai, who asked the Lord, 'Please, show me your glory' (Ex. 33:18). One thing matters.

What about evangelism? What about serving others? What about fellowship? Justice for the oppressed? Care for widows and orphans? Compassion for the suffering? Yes, those are all hallmarks of following Jesus. But what I am arguing in this book is that if we can see God, the very sight of Him will fuel and motivate all of those other things. As Paul tells us, when we behold God's glory, it will change everything about us (2 Cor. 3:18).

CHAPTER 1

NO ONE HAS EVER SEEN GOD

'What does God look like?' This sentence came out of my son Owen's mouth as he was lying down for bed one night. I think he was about five years old. My wife and I had just read the Bible and prayed with him and his little sister, so his little wheels were turning about the mysteries of God. How would you answer?

Ironically, in a book all about the pursuit to see God, we begin with the biblical principle that you can't. Twice in our New Testaments the Apostle John tells us, in no uncertain terms, 'No one has ever seen God' (John 1:18, 1 John 4:12). Consider the scope of those two identical statements. Of all the people who have ever lived, no one has seen Him. Of all the moments in history and all the interactions with God, none have resulted in someone catching even a glimpse. And this is no isolated doctrine. If you pay attention as you read your Bible, you will find a number of other biblical authors making a similar claim. You will even hear it from God Himself.

The first reason no one has ever seen God is that He is a spirit being. He has no physical form. God is invisible. This is part of what I tried (and probably failed) to communicate to my son Owen years ago. Paul writes to Timothy and says, 'To the King of the ages, immortal, *invisible*, the only God, be honor and glory forever

13

and ever. Amen' (1 Tim. 1:17, emphasis added). He says the same in places like Colossians 1:15 and Romans 1:20. In the modern Western world, many of us take this for granted, but in the days of Moses or Daniel or Paul, gods could be seen, touched, even placed on a mantle in the living room. It seems as though it is human nature to seek to visualize what we worship. Yet God sets Himself apart from all other false gods in that He does not allow Himself to be seen. (In chapter three we will discuss the question of making images of the invisible God.)

However, it is not simply that no one *has* seen this God, but that no one *can* see Him. Again, from Paul's first letter to Timothy, we read of God, 'who alone has immortality, who dwells in unapproachable light, *whom no one has ever seen or can see*' (1 Tim. 6:16, emphasis added). You could not see God even if you tried. Indeed, many have tried and failed. Human beings cannot simply travel to His dwelling place, but even if we could reach it, we would not be able to see Him. The light of His being is unapproachable. It's like trying to stare down a midday summer sun. Your eyes simply cannot take it. God and His dwelling place are like that— only infinitely more so.

We also see Jesus speaking of this to the Jews after they began to grumble about His comments that He was the true manna from heaven. Most Jews who knew their Old Testament stories would have been shocked and scandalized to hear a man claim that He was the fulfillment of the manna, the ultimate truth to which God was pointing. But Jesus goes on to make an even more extravagant claim—that He has seen God when no one else has! In John 6:45-46, Jesus says, 'Everyone who has heard and learned from the Father comes to me—*not that anyone has seen the Father* except he who is from God; he has seen the Father' (emphasis added). So, perhaps we must make one qualification to all we have said above. There is one who has seen God, but considering that this One is the Son of God, the second person of the Trinity, it would still be completely appropriate to say with John, 'No one has ever seen God' (John 1:18).

But what about…

At this point, someone might raise an objection. *What about times in the Bible where it seems someone did see God?* Yes, there are such events recorded in the Old Testament. Take Exodus 24:9-11 for example: 'Then Moses and Aaron, Nadab, and Abihu, and seventy of the elders of Israel went up, *and they saw the God of Israel.* There was under his feet as it were a pavement of sapphire stone, like the very heaven for clearness. And he did not lay his hand on the chief men of the people of Israel; they beheld God, and ate and drank' (emphasis added).

Does it not explicitly say 'they saw God'? Are the books of John and Exodus in conflict with one another? Have we found a genuine contradiction in Scripture? Here it is crucial for us to understand that Moses, Aaron, and the other Israelite leaders did not see God in His fullness or in His pure glory. The invisible God made Himself known to them in a way they could behold visually. He condescended to give them a unique experience of Himself that the rest of Israel did not witness, but they did not see God in His fullness—they couldn't. Moses learned this on that very same mountain, just a few chapters after the event mentioned above (more on this in chapter two).

We find other similar moments throughout the Old Testament where it seems as though someone saw God, and yet a closer examination reveals it was yet another example of God's gracious self-manifestation in a veiled form. We may think of God's special presence with Adam and Eve in the Garden of Eden (Gen. 3:8), or His appearance to Abraham by the oaks of Mamre (Gen. 18:1). Consider Moses' unique relationship with the Lord, as seen in Exodus 33:11, 'Thus the Lord used to speak to Moses face to face, as a man speaks to his friend.' Or, Numbers 12:8, where God says of Moses, 'With Him I speak mouth to mouth, clearly, and not in riddles, and he beholds the form of the Lord.' While the rest of Israel received God's Word through Moses as a mediator or prophet, Moses spoke with God directly. No wonder the people became jealous! These are yet more examples of God manifesting Himself to human beings in a form they can behold, but it is not His unveiled glory, or His true essence. Jack Cottrell, in his book *What the Bible Says About God the Creator*, writes,

> On these and other occasions God took upon himself a human form for the purpose of manifesting himself to various persons. Such manifestations are called *theophanies*, or appearances of God. The bodies in which he appeared were real human bodies, probably created *ex nihilo* [from nothing] for the short duration of the theophany and then

dissolved back into nothingness. In this way the Lord, who is invisible to our eyes as spirit, could be seen temporarily in a concrete form.[1]

Prophets in the Old Testament were sometimes given visions of the Lord. Micaiah (1 Kings 22:19; 2 Chr. 18:18), Isaiah (Is. 6:1-5), and Amos (Amos 1:9) all received a prophetic vision of God that accompanied His words to them. Yet, once again, none saw the full glory or undiluted form of God. Each vision was yet another gracious condescension from the Lord. As John Stott put it, 'The Old Testament theophanies were revelations either of God's glory or of God-in-disguise ("the angel of the Lord" appearing as a man); they were not visions of God as he is in himself.'[2]

The God Who Gives Us Himself

Episodes like these show us the kindness and benevolence of God toward His people. Every now and then He would manifest His presence to certain people to increase their faith, or to magnify Himself in their hearts and minds, or to motivate them to take His tough words to others. In fact, when we stop and think about it, the elaborate instructions God gave the Israelites for the tabernacle, and later the temple, were means by which a form of God's presence could dwell in the midst of His people. Time and time again we see God taking the initiative to give His people a glimpse of Himself.

In this we see His heart. God wants to give Himself to us! But why? Fundamentally, it is in God's very nature to be self-giving. You cannot begin to describe or understand God properly without understanding the concept that His goodness and power and life overflow to others. This helps us to understand what the Apostle John meant when he wrote, 'God is love' (1 John 4:8, 16). What is love if not a giving of oneself to others for their good? This is what God *is*. This is His essence. And He has created us in such a way that our greatest satisfaction and joy can only be found in Him.

The whole reason I have written this book is to stir up your longing for God. No one has ever seen God, in His full glory, with their physical eyes. But that is not what we are after. Seeing God

---

1. Jack Cottrell, *What the Bible Says About God the Creator: The Doctrine of God*, vol. 1 (Eugene: Wipf & Stock, 1983), 230-231.

2. John R.W. Stott, *The Letters of John: An Introduction and Commentary* (Downers Grove: InterVarsity, 1988), Vol. 19, 164.

means experiencing and beholding Him. In that way He is pleased to give us His glory in proportion to the level of our hunger and thirst for it. Let me repeat that because I don't want you to read over it and miss it. *God is pleased to give us His glory in proportion to the level of our hunger and thirst for it.* My overarching goal in writing this book is to stir our hearts up to seek God Himself, over and above all of His good gifts and blessings, as the ultimate reward of Christianity.

David wrote, 'Delight yourself in the Lord, and he will give you the desires of your heart' (Ps. 37:4). This does not mean that delight in God is a means by which we can get something else that we desire. It is not a way to manipulate God into giving you what you really want, perhaps money or comfort or possessions. The greatest desire of your heart is God! So, as David says, delight yourself in Him and you will have the desire of your heart. Augustine famously said, 'For you have made us for yourself, and our heart is restless until it rests in you.'[3] In His lovingkindness, our heavenly Father has created us in such a way that our heart cannot rest until it has its greatest desire—God. As Paul told the Athenians in Acts 17:27, God created human beings 'that they should seek God, and perhaps feel their way toward Him and find Him. Yet he is actually not far from each one of us.'

No one has ever seen God, and no one will until we behold His glory in eternity. Even then, considering God is an invisible being, we will still need Him to reveal Himself to us in a form we can visually behold. But until then, He continually invites us to experience Him, to know Him, and to find satisfaction in Him alone. He longs to give us Himself. As A. W. Tozer once wrote, 'Our pursuit of God is successful just because He is forever seeking to manifest Himself to us.'[4] In our day He has given us Himself in many non-visual forms, but the principle remains: God is always, actively providing a way for His people to experience His presence to satisfy their heart's greatest desire.

---

3. Saint Augustine, *The Confessions of St. Augustine*, trans. John K. Ryan (New York: Image Books, 1988), 1.

4. A. W. Tozer, *The Pursuit of God* (Bloomington: Bethany House, 2013), Kindle loc. 722.

CHAPTER 2

YOU CANNOT SEE GOD AND LIVE

Do you want to see God? Perhaps you think if you saw Him you would never be the same again. You would be right. Perhaps you think it would make you happier than you've ever been in your whole life. Well, if you are a Christian, you would be right. Perhaps you think everything else in life would fade away because of His all-consuming glory. Again, you would be right. That's because you would be dead.

In chapter one we examined the biblical teaching that no one has ever seen God. God is invisible and dwells in unapproachable light. It is impossible for human beings to see God in His essence or His unveiled glory.

Perhaps the one man in history who understood this principle best (other than Jesus, of course) was Moses. You may recall Moses' first encounter with God in Exodus 3. God spoke to Moses from a burning bush which was located at Horeb, a place described as 'the mountain of God' (Ex. 3:1). Horeb was another name for Mount Sinai. As Moses listened to the voice of the Lord coming from the bush, little did he know that after the ten plagues and the Red Sea crossing, God would lead him and his fellow Israelites back to that same mountain for another life-changing encounter.

Moses' conversation with God on Mount Sinai in Exodus chapters 32–34 is one of the most fascinating passages in all the Bible. Twice in these chapters God makes a declaration to Moses of how He intends to punish the Israelites, and twice Moses successfully intercedes for the people. First, God announces He will destroy the people for worshiping the golden calf. Moses intercedes and begs God for mercy. God relents. Next, God announces He will not go with them as they travel to the Promised Land because of their stubbornness. Moses again intercedes and begs for God to accompany them. God graciously agrees. The favor and honor given to Moses by God in these exchanges is quite surprising. Moses serves as a wonderful example for us of striving with God in prayer. Decades earlier, when God changed Jacob's name to Israel after their epic wrestling match, He said to him, 'for you have striven with God and with men, and have prevailed' (Gen. 32:28). But it would be quite reasonable to say that Moses, even more so than Jacob, strove with God and prevailed.

However, this was not enough for Moses. You would expect, after all this, for Moses to quit while he was ahead. God had graciously and surprisingly granted his two bold requests. Surely he had used up all his favor with the Lord. Surely he had no more claim on God's generosity. It's not hard to picture Moses opening his mouth, ready to ask for more, before God interrupts him and says, 'Don't push it, Moses.' Yet that is exactly what Moses does.

In one of the most God-centered prayer requests in all of Scripture, Moses says, 'Please, show me your glory' (Ex. 33:18). You see, Moses wanted God more than anything. If God would not go with them to the Promised Land, none of the comforts and pleasures of that place would be worth it. Moses' example here is something I think all Christians are striving for. We want to reach a point where we could not imagine life—even eternal life—without God as our portion, our reward. Moses longed for the Lord more than any of His gifts. And it is God's response to his wonderful request that provides us with our focus for this chapter.

God tells Moses He will hide him in a cleft of the mountain, cover him with His hand, and pass by, proclaiming His name, or His glory (you will find the Bible hardly differentiates the two), in the hearing of Moses. Then God says He will remove His hand, so that Moses may see His back. 'But,' God says, 'you cannot see my face, *for man shall not see me and live*' (Ex. 33:20, emphasis added).

Right there God revealed a fundamental, indeed monumental, principle of His interactions with human beings, and we need to pause to consider its implications. You cannot see God and live to tell about it.

Written on Our Hearts

Ever since I first read that exchange, I have been absolutely enthralled by it. So much so that over the years I have come to notice other places in Scripture where men and women seem to intuitively understand this principle—that no one may see God and live—without God even having to inform them of it.

Take Jacob, for example. We have already briefly mentioned his wrestling match with God in Genesis 32. The entire passage (verses 22-32) is densely packed with deep theological truths and implications for our lives today, (and did I mention it's a *wrestling match with God?!*). But for our purposes here I want to draw your attention to what Jacob did immediately after the encounter. He named the place *Peniel*, a word which means 'the face of God,' and we are told he chose this name for a reason: 'For I have seen God face to face, and yet my life has been delivered' (Gen. 32:30).

Initially this might seem like it poses a problem, considering God told Moses that no one could see His face and live. However, when God spoke those words to Moses, He meant something of what we saw in chapter one, namely that no one may see God's unveiled glory. God does not literally have a face, or a back for that matter, or arms (Is. 59:1), or hands (Job 19:21). He is Spirit (John 4:24). He has no human body. When God speaks of His face, He means His essence, or His pure form. No one may see *that* and live. Jack Cottrell writes, 'Because it was not his true essence, those who saw him did not die as they expected.'[1] Jacob saw God 'face to face' in the same way Moses would speak with God 'face to face' (see Ex. 33:11 and Deut. 34:10). God revealed Himself to Jacob in a way that would not destroy him.

But notice how Jacob intuitively understood that he should be dead, not as a result of wrestling God, but from merely *seeing Him*! God did not inform him of this. He just knew it. And he is not the only one in Scripture who just knew. The Israelite people seemed to understand this when they saw the presence of God

---

1. Cottrell, *God the Creator*, 231.

surrounding Mount Sinai in a dark cloud with fire and thunder. Deuteronomy 5 records their words.

> Behold, the Lord our God has shown us his glory and greatness, and we have heard his voice out of the midst of the fire. This day we have seen God speak with man, and man still live. Now therefore why should we die? For this great fire will consume us. If we hear the voice of the Lord our God anymore, we shall die. For who is there of all flesh, that has heard the voice of the living God speaking out of the midst of fire as we have, and has still lived? (Deut. 5:24-26)

The Israelites only saw a raw representation of God as smoke and fire covering the mountain, yet after hearing His voice and understanding whose presence it was that covered the mountain, their God-given instincts told them they should have died.

Gideon understood this as well. In Judges 6, Gideon has an encounter with a figure known as *the angel of the Lord*. A closer study of the Old Testament appearances of this enigmatic figure will reveal He is more than your typical angel. He is a divine manifestation of God Himself (more on this later). But notice Gideon's concern once he realizes who he is dealing with: 'Then Gideon perceived that he was the angel of the Lord. And Gideon said, "Alas, O Lord God! For now I have seen the angel of the Lord face to face." But the Lord said to him, "Peace be to you. *Do not fear; you shall not die*"' (Judg. 6:22-23, emphasis added). We see from God's reassuring response that Gideon feared for his life because of what he had seen. He instinctively understood, man may not see God and live. Samson's parents voice the same intuitive fear in Judges 13:22.

In a less obvious example we find Hagar, the servant of Abraham and Sarah, expressing astonishment that she has just seen the Lord and yet has been spared. The New American Standard Bible translation of Genesis 16:13 captures her words best: 'Have I even remained alive here after seeing Him?' Whereas other translations miss this aspect of the passage, both Derek Kidner in his Genesis commentary, and Robert Alter, an expert in biblical Hebrew, argue that this detail should not be missed when translating this passage into English.[2]

---

2. Derek Kidner, *Genesis: An Introduction and Commentary*, vol. 1, Tyndale Old Testament Commentaries (Downers Grove, IL: InterVarsity Press, 1967), 138.

What is strikingly common among all of these encounters is that these men and women, who saw a manifestation of God, all instinctively knew, without God having to tell them, that they should be dead. It is as though God has written this principle on our hearts. There is a fundamental separation between human beings and the Almighty God, and we all know it.

The Holiness of God

What is it about God that would kill us if we saw Him? Paul wrote to Timothy that God dwells in 'unapproachable light' (1 Tim. 6:16). Does this mean the brightness of God's glory is so intense it would be too much for our finite bodies to handle? Is this simply a principle of physics? Perhaps so. It would make complete sense that our current bodies do not have the capacity to behold such an intense and overwhelming energy source. Perhaps one reason God will give us new bodies for eternity is so that we can be near Him without exploding!

But I think there is something more. The most likely answer comes from the biblical truth of God's holiness and our sinfulness. Throughout Scripture, God tells us that He is holy, which simply means *set apart*. He is different from all of creation. While everything else is created, He is the uncreated creator, having always existed from eternity past. Every created thing is dependent upon Him for its existence whereas God has life in Himself (John 5:26). But most relevant to our topic in this chapter, God is completely without sin, while every human being is sinful. And because of God's perfect purity and righteousness, He opposes all sin to the fullest extent. It is His very nature to do so. Just as we saw in chapter one that God *is* love, the book of *Hebrews* tells us 'our God is a consuming fire' (Heb. 10:29). His opposition to sin is an extension of His holiness, and this opposition manifests itself in wrath. When sin comes into the presence of this perfectly holy and righteous God it is quickly consumed by His wrath.

This is why we cannot see God and live. Sinners cannot come into the unveiled presence of a holy God without being consumed by His wrath. There is perhaps no clearer example of this principle in all of Scripture than Leviticus 10:1-3, where Aaron's two sons,

---

Robert Alter, *The Hebrew Bible, Vol. 1: The Five Books of Moses* (New York: W.W. Norton & Co, 2019), 53.

Nadab and Abihu, offered 'unauthorized fire' before the Lord. We read that immediately, 'fire came out from before the Lord and consumed them, and they died before the Lord' (verse 2). Sinful human beings cannot simply come before the Lord in whatever way they please. The consequences are fatal. As pastor Luke Walker said, 'The sun will burn your eyes out from 92 million miles away, and you expect to casually stroll into the presence of its creator?'[3]

A Merciful Gift of Grace

As we have already seen, God has written this principle on our hearts. We know it intuitively. When God appeared to men and women in the Old Testament, they would come away marveling at the fact that their lives had been spared. At first, this implanted knowledge might seem like a curse from God. If this is the way things are, why would He appear to some, here and there, and give us all the dread of knowing that any encounter should destroy us? Why not simply withdraw His presence and spare us the uneasiness? In actuality, this knowledge is a gracious gift.

Our natural understanding that everyone who sees God deserves death is actually one of the many imbedded truths that God uses to draw us to Himself and to His Son Jesus. In Acts 17, when Paul is speaking to the men of Athens about the existence of the one true God, he tells them that God has created human beings in such a way, 'that they should seek God, and perhaps feel their way toward him and find him. Yet he is actually not far from each one of us' (Acts 17:27). He has put eternity in our hearts to give each person an intuitive knowledge that there is life after death (Ecc. 3:11). He has revealed Himself in creation to the point that every human being on earth has a rudimentary knowledge of God's existence and His rightful claim to our honor and gratitude (Rom. 1:19-21). He has written a law of morality on our hearts that even pagans can perceive (Rom. 2:14-15). And He has created each one of us with an understanding that to see Him in all His holiness, righteousness, and purity would result in our death.

You do not have to pick up a Bible to learn these truths. You have them in your heart by default. Unfortunately, this knowledge is not enough to save you—it is only enough to condemn you.

---

3. Luke Walker, Twitter Post. August 21, 2017, 10:02 AM. https://twitter.com/spiritualswords/status/899647780368592896

Nevertheless, it is enough to begin the process of awakening you to your need to be reconciled to God. God has graciously given every single person enough knowledge to drive them to seek a solution... a solution that can only be found within the pages of the Bible.

CHAPTER 3

THE SECOND COMMANDMENT

Our kids have been drawing and painting pictures of my wife and me for years now. When they were very young, we were the most basic stick figures with smiley faces. As our kids have gotten a bit older, the pictures have become more and more detailed and slightly more realistic. In professional art (which I sometimes have difficulty distinguishing from toddler art) there are also varying levels of how realistic a painting might appear. Works of the impressionistic or painterly styles clearly look like paintings with visible brush strokes. On the other end of the spectrum, though, is photorealism, in which the artist takes extraordinary pains to make his or her painting look like an actual photograph, even down to the smallest of details. Just the other day I saw an online picture of a Michael Jordan rookie card in clear high definition, only later to realize it was a phenomenal photorealistic painting by an artist named Graig Kreindler.[1]

The question is this: How accurately can an image portray the reality? While the sweet scribbles of our toddlers are precious treasures to parents, they are not very good representations of what is really there. Photorealism, on the other hand, pushes the boundaries of the level of accuracy that can be achieved by an artist.

---

1.   Graig Kreindler, Twitter Post. September 24, 2020, 7:33 PM. https://twitter.com/GraigKreindler/status/1309289968263737350

In our quest to see God, not only are we confronted by the fact that God does not allow Himself to be seen, but also that God forbids us from trying to portray Him in any kind of image. This is the essence of the second of the Ten Commandments. 'You shall not make for yourself a carved image, or any likeness of anything that is in heaven above, or that is in the earth beneath, or that is in the water under the earth.' (Ex. 20:4) The King James Version memorably uses the phrase 'graven images,' which refers specifically to images carved (or en*graved*) in stone, wood, or metal, but it also includes the phrase 'or any likeness.' In other words, God says we must not seek to visually represent Him in any physical form that we can see or imagine. You might say, as we saw in chapter one, the second commandment forbids us from trying to make the invisible God visible.

Distorting and Diminishing

While the first commandment forbids us from worshiping other false gods or idols, the second commandment prohibits us from worshiping the true God in a false or inappropriate manner. Depicting God in any kind of visual form is a sin against His very nature because God is spirit (John 4:24). He may take a visual form as He so chooses, and temporarily manifest Himself to someone in what is known as a theophany, but for us to decide for ourselves what visual form should best represent Him is an act of spiritual arrogance and indifference to His holiness and His transcendence.

When we say God is holy or transcendent, we mean He is completely set apart from all other created things. He is utterly unique and therefore unlike anything we could use to visually represent Him. Trying to depict God in any visual form is wrong because it will always distort and diminish our view of Him in numerous ways. Any representation that we can imagine, fashion, or see will inevitably leave out important aspects of God's character and His nature. No statue or picture or video can capture the fullness of His glory, and therefore any attempt to do so would demean or belittle it. As God says in Isaiah, 'To whom then will you liken God, or what likeness compare with him?' (Is. 40:18). Notice the use, once again, of the word *likeness*. It will play a significant role in later chapters as we examine other aspects of seeing God.

Consider also the words of Paul in Romans 1 where he speaks of those who, 'exchanged the glory of the immortal God for images resembling mortal man and birds and animals and creeping things' (Rom. 1:23). This, perhaps, was Aaron's primary sin during the golden calf incident in Exodus 32. After collecting the gold and jewelry from the people and having it fashioned into a golden calf, the people say, 'These are your gods, O Israel, who brought you up out of the land of Egypt!' But in the very next verse, Aaron proclaims, 'Tomorrow shall be a feast to the Lord' (Ex. 32:4-5). The text is not definitive, but it seems possible that Aaron was trying to get the people to use the golden calf as a visual aid to worship the Lord. Yet if this were true it would not exonerate him, because even if he were not breaking the first of the Ten Commandments, he was most definitely breaking the second. It is not difficult to think of all the ways a golden calf would distort and diminish the worshiper's idea of the almighty, transcendent God of the Bible.

It is crucial not to miss God's words to Moses immediately following the second commandment. 'You shall not bow down to them or serve them, *for I the Lord your God am a jealous God*, visiting the iniquity of the fathers on the children to the third and the fourth generation of those who hate me, but showing steadfast love to thousands of those who love me and keep my commandments' (Ex. 20:5-6, emphasis added). After handing down this commandment to Moses, and before moving on to the next one, God takes time to explain His own jealousy.

Does the fact that God calls Himself jealous rub you the wrong way? You would not be the first. People often bristle at these verses because jealousy among human beings is hardly ever seen as a virtue. It's a selfish vice to be avoided at all costs. Is God like the controlling husband who refuses to let his wife speak to other men? Is He like the high school girl who desperately wishes she could have the looks and popularity of her friend the homecoming queen?

This is not what God means when He says He is jealous. It is much more like the faithful wife who refuses to share her husband with another woman. Her love for him is exclusive and she rightly believes his love for her should be the same. If another woman were seeking to draw his heart away from their marriage, she would be right to stand up and do whatever it takes to protect the sanctity of their covenant with one another. In the same way, God is jealous for His people. He will not share us with another. We are either committed to Him one hundred percent, or not at all. To split our devotion to God with other false deities is, according to Scripture, spiritual adultery.

This jealousy also reveals to us how serious God is about how He is represented. He is passionately concerned that He is worshiped in the right way, and that He not be depicted inaccurately. He does not take being misrepresented lightly! This is a big part of the reason why He speaks of His jealousy immediately after giving this second commandment. The commandment is grounded in the fact that God is jealous for His people, not only that they worship Him exclusively, but also accurately.

Paintings of Jesus and Children's Bibles

If it is sinful to visually represent God, then it would be natural to wonder about artistic expressions depicting Jesus and His ministry or His death. Are these sinful as well? Throughout church history, believers have been on both sides of this issue. On the one hand, many hold the conviction that the second commandment not only prohibits us from making images of God the Father but of any person within the Trinity, including the Son. While Christ Himself was a visible image of God on earth, the incarnation was God's doing, not man's. Images of Christ, however, are our own creations and thus are prone to distorting and diminishing, as just discussed.

On the other hand, there are those who would argue that because Jesus was a human being with a physical body who, during His time on this earth, was seen by thousands of people, depictions of Him would not violate the second commandment. As we will see in the next chapter, God intentionally chose to represent Himself visually in the form of the man, Jesus of Nazareth. The Bible tells us very little about the details of His physical appearance, but from my perspective artistic depictions do not break the second commandment for the same reason the incarnation itself did not do so.

While I do not agree, I sympathize with those in the first group and I fully respect their convictions. It is a biblically-defensible position and it is wise to err on the side of caution when it comes to debatable matters. Personally, I have no reservations enjoying classic works of art, kids books, or films and TV shows depicting the life and death of Jesus. I would, however, draw the line at using these depictions for worship.

I also believe it is important for those of us in the second group to be alert to the danger of becoming dependent upon these visual aides to stir our affections for Christ and His glory. The primary way God has ordained for us to see the glory of Christ is through the eyes of our hearts. We are to behold Him by faith, not by sight. Even during His time on earth, there were those who saw Him and His miracles with their physical eyes, but did not behold His glory in their hearts. Beware of becoming dependent upon images, works of art, or films and television shows to stir your affections for Christ. These may have their place, but the revelation of Christ through God's inspired word, the Bible, must be primary. If we do not consistently seek His glory through Scripture, our faith muscles will slowly atrophy, and our ability to treasure Him in our hearts could disappear altogether. Do not trade the inner, transforming power of the Spirit for outward stimulants.

A God in Our Own Image

Earlier I said we must not seek to visually represent God in any physical form that we can imagine. Note the root word *image* in *imagine*. In the second commandment God forbids us to make or fashion an image to represent Him in visual form, but those images are the result of human beings trying to imagine what God would or should look like. The problem with this is God is beyond anything we can imagine because our imaginations are forced to draw on things we have seen, and no one has ever seen God! The late A. W. Tozer once wrote, 'we begin to think of God in terms of our limitations... we end up with a caricature of God, a God that is not worthy of our worship. Too many people are worshiping the God of their own imaginations.'[2]

Most of us have probably heard someone say something to this effect: 'I like to think of God as...' or even, 'I can't imagine God would ever...' This is an all-too-common way of breaking the second commandment. When we hear the second commandment, we typically think of statues or pictures, things we can see or touch. But we should also understand it as forbidding us to create an image of God in our own minds apart from His self-revelation in the Bible.

---

2. A. W. Tozer, *Delighting in God* (Bloomington: Bethany House, 2015), 114.

If it is sinful to imagine God in a certain way and then depict that as a statue or picture, it seems clear that the first act of imagining would be in itself sinful. I would argue that the primary way those in our modern, western civilization break the second commandment is forming an idea of God in their mind that has been informed by something other than God's own words about Himself.

Remember, when compared with all of creation, God is in a category of His own. He is transcendent and holy, completely set apart. He is infinite and incomprehensible, entirely more than we can fathom. This means for mankind to know Him, He must tell us about Himself. Thankfully, He has done so clearly and sufficiently in His Word, the Bible. In fact, that is primarily what the Bible is—a book of God's revelation about Himself and how people ought to respond. God must tell us who He is. I have always found it astounding that a human being, having only lived twenty or thirty-some years on the earth, having only ever dwelt among a small fraction of the earth's population, can have the audacity to create their own ideas of the transcendent God based on little more than their own guesses and feelings. And yet, I consistently hear people say things like, 'I just don't think God would ever send a good person to hell...' or 'I like to think of God as someone who is always there when we need Him but doesn't really interfere in our lives.' To think that we can define God apart from His own words about Himself is the pinnacle of human arrogance and ignorance.

But perhaps there is more going on in the hearts of those who make such statements than can be seen on the surface. The great Anglican theologian J. I. Packer says, 'We know from experience how often remarks of this kind serve as the prelude to a denial of something that the Bible tells us about God.'[3] In other words, it may not be legitimate ignorance so much as a willful attempt to avoid and suppress the truth (Rom. 1:18).

To those who have yet to repent and humble themselves under His mighty hand, true knowledge of God comes not as a comfort, but as a threat to their own comfort. In John 3, Jesus said, 'And this is the judgment: the light has come into the world, and people loved the darkness rather than the light because their works were evil. For everyone who does wicked things hates the light and does not come to the light, lest his works should be exposed' (John 3:19-20).

---

3.   J. I. Packer, *Knowing God* (Downers Grove: InterVarsity Press, 1973), 47.

In other words, the problem is not a lack of knowledge but a lack of humility. People refuse to come to Jesus, not because the evidence is less than compelling, but because of their deep love for sin. Deep down we know that following Jesus means denying ourselves and taking up our cross. We know it means repentance, forsaking our sin, and putting to death the deeds of the body. It's like a hoarder agreeing to be the subject of one of those television shows. If you let Jesus in, He's going to start cleaning the house, and it will be quite uncomfortable at first.

So, we see that in the second commandment God is not merely forbidding us to depict Him in things we can see or touch. He is also commanding us not to create an image of Him in our own minds apart from His own self-revelation in the Bible. He is commanding us not to create a god in our own image. Genesis 1:26-27 says that God created us in His image. The second commandment is essentially God's way of telling us not to reverse that process. God is saying, '*I create you in my image, not the other way around.*'

We have seen that God will not allow us to create our own visual representations of Him. He forbids us to make our own images. In the next two chapters we turn our attention to the two primary ways God has chosen His own images, His own visual representations: Jesus, and human beings.

CHAPTER 4

SEEING GOD IN JESUS CHRIST

'Has anyone ever told you you look like Tony Hawk?' Believe it or
not, the man himself, the greatest skateboarder of all time, hears this
quite often. He's right in front of them, but all kinds of people who
supposedly know who the skateboarding legend is fail to recognize
him. Hawk's Twitter feed is filled with hilarious, real-life stories
of folks mistaking him for himself. The funniest ones are the TSA
agents at the airport who are staring right at his ID!

It was the same in Jesus' day. Those who were made through Him
did not know Him. His own did not receive Him (John 1:10-11).
Ironically, so many who claimed to know God did not recognize
Him when He showed up in their midst! Why? Two reasons: their
hearts were not truly open to Him, and they did not expect Him to
show Himself in this particular way. Martyn Lloyd-Jones, one of
the most renowned preachers and authors of modern church history,
once wrote, '"Show me thy glory," cries humanity. And God says,
"I will show you my glory, but in my own way. And this is the
way—in the face of Jesus Christ."'[1]

The Apostle John writes, 'No one has ever seen God; the
only God, who is at the Father's side, he has made him known'

---

1. D. Martyn Lloyd-Jones, *Revival* (Wheaton: Crossway, 1987), Kindle loc.
4,442.

(John 1:18). This verse serves as a fitting end to the prologue of John's gospel account. In John 1:18, he goes on to tell us that even though we have not directly seen God the Father, we have seen Him in His only son, Jesus Christ. Paul tells us Jesus is how the invisible God has chosen to make Himself visible (Col. 1:15), and the author of Hebrews tells us that God made Christ an exact imprint, or stamp, of His nature.

Jesus' time on this earth is the closest human beings will ever get to seeing God on this side of eternity. And His life was such a wonderfully accurate portrayal of the heart, mind, and work of the Father that we are in no way left disappointed. Philip learned this during his conversation with Jesus the night before the crucifixion. In John 14, Jesus tells His disciples, 'I am the way, and the truth, and the life. No one comes to the Father except through me. If you had known me, you would have known my Father also. From now on you do know him and have seen him.' (John 14:6-7) Philip replies by saying, 'Lord, show us the Father, and it is enough for us.'

The text does not tell us Philip's heart in this request to Jesus, so we need to be careful not to be too definitive or dogmatic in our conclusions here. It is vitally important that we never go beyond what the Bible tells us (1 Cor. 4:6) or add to it in any way (Rev. 22:18). However, it can be helpful to make some educated guesses. It could be that Philip is confused by Jesus having just said they have seen the Father. Philip would have been quite certain he had *not* seen God, but instead of trying to correct Jesus, he simply asks for Him to show them the Father. Or perhaps Philip trusts that what Jesus is saying is true, but he desires to see more of God, much like Moses saying, 'Please show me your glory,' in Exodus 33. Either way, do not miss Philip's desire to see God. Philip understands what I hope you are beginning to see as you read this book: if we can behold the glory of God, everything will change. As New Testament scholar D.A. Carson says, 'He (Philip) thus joins the queue of human beings through the ages who have rightly understood that there can be no higher experience, no greater good, than seeing God as he is, in unimaginable splendour and transcendent glory.'[2]

Jesus responds to Philip's request by saying,

---

2. D.A. Carson, *The Gospel According to John* (Grand Rapids: Eerdmans, 1991), 494.

Have I been with you so long, and you still do not know me, Philip? Whoever has seen me has seen the Father. How can you say, "Show us the Father"? Do you not believe that I am in the Father and the Father is in me? The words that I say to you I do not speak on my own authority, but the Father who dwells in me does his works (John 14:9-10).

In other words, those who watched Jesus as He lived saw God the Father. They saw Him in Jesus' words and His works. They saw Him because, as Jesus said, 'I am in the Father and the Father is in me.'

Jesus Is God

This is much more than someone saying they see my Dad in me. I might remind them of my Dad, but in the end, we are two different people. But the connection between God the Father and God the Son is so fundamental that when you see one you see the other. The majestic and mind-bending truth of the incarnation is that Jesus, the Son of God, is also God the Son, the second person of the Trinity. 'In the beginning was the Word, and the Word was with God, and the Word was God' (John 1:1). It is simultaneously true that He was *with* God and that He *was* God. One God, three persons: Father, Son, and Holy Spirit.

As Jesus began to reveal to the Jews who He was and what He had come to do, they began to realize the audacity of His claims. He was claiming to be God in the flesh. Jesus' exchange with some of the Jews in John 8 is particularly striking.

'Truly, truly, I say to you, if anyone keeps my word, he will never see death.' The Jews said to him, 'Now we know that you have a demon! Abraham died, as did the prophets, yet you say, "If anyone keeps my word, he will never taste death." Are you greater than our father Abraham, who died? And the prophets died! Who do you make yourself out to be?' Jesus answered, 'If I glorify myself, my glory is nothing. It is my Father who glorifies me, of whom you say, "He is our God." But you have not known him. I know him. If I were to say that I do not know him, I would be a liar like you, but I do know him and I keep his word. Your father Abraham rejoiced that he would see my day. He saw it and was glad.' So the Jews said to him, 'You are not yet fifty years old, and

have you seen Abraham?' Jesus said to them, 'Truly, truly,
I say to you, before Abraham was, I am.' So they picked up
stones to throw at him, but Jesus hid himself and went out
of the temple. (John 8:51-59)

Jesus knew full well the weight and the honor the Jews gave to
Abraham and the Old Testament prophets. Therefore, He also
knew full well that these words would scandalize and offend
many who heard them. There were times in Jesus' ministry when
He intentionally spoke in ways that would push some away
and draw others in, depending on the openness of their hearts. This
is a prime example.

Notice specifically what Jesus said to them in John 8:58, 'Before
Abraham was, I am,' and how they immediately picked up stones to
stone Him. Why did they do this? Because they understood what He
was claiming about Himself. Do you remember when God spoke
to Moses through the burning bush and told him to go to Pharaoh
and demand the freedom of God's people? Moses knew his fellow
Israelites might be skeptical of him. Perhaps they may not believe
God actually spoke to him. What should Moses tell them if they ask
for the name of this God who sent him? God responded by telling
Moses His name: 'I am who I am... Say this to the people of Israel:
"I am has sent me to you"' (Ex. 3:14). The Hebrew words behind 'I
AM WHO I AM' are where we get the name YAHWEH. This is
God's name: 'I AM.' There is nothing greater you could say about
Him. He simply is. He is the self-existent one.

So then, when Jesus said to the Jews, 'Before Abraham was, I
am,' they immediately understood the implications, and they picked
up stones to stone Him. Why? For blasphemy, of course. This was
a man that had just claimed to be God! And, if this had been any
other man, His words would indeed have been blasphemous. But
not for Jesus. He truly is God in the flesh... God with us.

We see a similar situation play out when Jesus said in John 10:30,
'I and the Father are one.' Again they picked up stones to stone
Him for claiming to be God. It was hard for many to accept, and it
remains so today, but this is the clear and consistent witness of the
New Testament.

John 20:28, Romans 9:5, Colossians 1:19 and 2:9, Titus 2:13,
Hebrews 1:8, and 2 Peter 1:2 all speak of Jesus as God. Even John's
claim that no one has ever seen God, speaks of Jesus as God: 'No

one has ever seen God; *the only God*, who is at the Father's side, he has made him known' (John 1:18, emphasis added). We see God in Jesus because Jesus is God incarnated as a human being.

To See God You Must Come Through Jesus

When God sent Jesus into the world it forever changed the way human beings would seek and see God. No longer was it enough to come to God through priests, sacrifices, or any of the old covenant laws. As Jesus told Philip, 'No one comes to the Father except through me' (John 14:6). The only way we will see God is if we seek Him through His Son Jesus Christ. Pursue Him in any other way and you will not find Him.

The Apostle John tells us, 'No one who denies the Son has the Father. Whoever confesses the Son has the Father also' (1 John 2:23). Can you imagine how controversial this would have been for first century Jews, whose families had followed the Old Testament law for generations? Now, all of a sudden, they are being told that if they do not ally themselves with this new teacher, and if they do not confess that He is the promised Messiah, they will be cut off from God!

These were hard words, no doubt, but not in the way we might initially think. Perhaps it might seem unfair for Jesus to abruptly upend generations of family tradition. How could He expect someone to quickly turn away from all that their loving parents and grandparents had taught them? Especially if those parents had been teaching them to know and love the one, true God?

Once again, let us return to Jesus' conversations with the Jews in John 8-10, where Jesus gives us an essential key to understanding God's clarified requirement for salvation—coming to Him through Jesus. When the Jews began to question Jesus' claims about Himself, He told them things like, 'If God were your Father, you would love me, for I came from God and I am here' (John 8:42), and also, 'The works that I do in my Father's name bear witness about me, but you do not believe because you are not among my sheep. My sheep hear my voice, and I know them, and they follow me' (John 10:25-27).[3]

What Jesus is saying here is that those who truly knew God welcomed Jesus and His words, while those who only claimed to know God on the surface, but did not actually know Him in their

---

3.   See also John 5:39-47; 7:17

hearts, rejected Jesus and His words. Before Jesus came onto the scene, the only ways to see and know God were through what He had revealed in creation to all people, which provides limited knowledge, and through His law, revealed only to the Israelites. The first, according to the Apostle Paul, provides only enough knowledge of God to condemn us (Rom. 1:18ff). But even for an Israelite, surface level law-keeping did not guarantee you a path to God. There were those who sought the Lord from the heart, but also those who kept the law superficially. There was a difference between being a Jew outwardly, and being one on the inside. As Paul says, 'For no one is a Jew who is merely one outwardly, nor is circumcision outward and physical. But a Jew is one inwardly, and circumcision is a matter of the heart, by the Spirit, not by the letter. His praise is not from man but from God' (Rom. 2:28-29).

In the first century, the Pharisees and others like them would have claimed that they knew God, but when God showed up in their midst they were offended and repulsed, revealing that they did not truly know God in the first place. On the other hand, those who were genuinely seeking God before Jesus showed up, as well as those whose hearts were truly open to Him, found themselves warmed and attracted to Jesus' message and His miracles. This is one of the primary reasons Jesus often taught using parables. In Matthew 13:10-17, Jesus explains to His disciples the purpose of His parables. Those with soft hearts open toward God would comprehend the truth in Jesus' stories, but those whose hearts were hard and closed to God—like the Pharisees—would be pushed farther away. As it has often been said, 'The same sun that melts the ice hardens the clay.' This is why Jesus taught that whoever loved God listened to Him, or that anyone who truly had God as their Father would love Jesus. Jesus was God in the flesh, so it makes perfect sense that those who knew God recognized Him in Jesus. As we have already noted, Jesus was the exact imprint of God's nature (Heb. 1:3) and 'the image of the invisible God' (Col. 1:15). So, when the Good Shepherd called, the true sheep, the true children of God, recognized His voice and came running. The other sheep heard the voice of a stranger and ran away.

And so, we see that it was in no way unreasonable for God to expect first century Jews to come to Him through Jesus. Those whose hearts were truly longing to see God saw Him when Jesus showed up. This can be seen in the story of one of the most interesting characters in John's gospel, Nicodemus. While most of the Pharisees feel threatened by Jesus as He rises to popularity, Nicodemus is instead drawn to Him. He comes to Jesus by night and confesses that he knows Jesus is a teacher who has come from God. Nicodemus has been longing to see God and His glory his entire life, and now that it is here, he is starting to recognize it. We know this was the beginning of Nicodemus's saving faith—or sight—because later in John's gospel, we see him helping to care for Jesus's body (John 19:39). Conversely, the reaction of the other Pharisees to Jesus' ministry shows they were not genuinely seeking God in the first place, but rather their own glory and comfort. Think of John the Baptist, whose heart must have felt like it was leaping out of his chest when he first laid eyes on Jesus and shouted, 'Behold, the Lamb of God, who takes away the sin of the world!' (John 1:29). Those who truly longed to see God recognized Him when He showed up.

So now that Jesus has come, we can only see God if we come to Him through Jesus. The myriad of religions in the world show us that human beings long to see God, but it cannot be done apart from Christ. Kevin DeYoung, a well-respected author, pastor and seminary professor, has rightly said,

> The implication from all this is that if you don't know God in Christ, then you don't really know God. The first commandment can no longer be properly obeyed unless we worship the one who alone shows us the one true God. It isn't enough to use the word God or to belong to a monotheistic religion. We are not worshiping the one true God unless we are worshiping the God and Father of our Lord Jesus Christ. The coming of Christ has changed everything.[4]

Seeing God at the Cross

It is not only in the life and teachings and miracles of Jesus that we clearly see God the Father, but it is also in His death. The cross is not simply a display of the glory and love of Jesus, but of God the Father as well. No other passage in Scripture captures this principle better than Romans 3:21-26:

---

4.   Kevin DeYoung, *The 10 Commandments* (Wheaton: Crossway, 2018), 33.

But now the righteousness of God has been manifested apart from the law, although the Law and the Prophets bear witness to it—the righteousness of God through faith in Jesus Christ for all who believe. For there is no distinction: for all have sinned and fall short of the glory of God, and are justified by his grace as a gift, through the redemption that is in Christ Jesus, whom God put forward as a propitiation by his blood, to be received by faith. This was to show God's righteousness, because in his divine forbearance he had passed over former sins. It was to show his righteousness at the present time, so that he might be just and the justifier of the one who has faith in Jesus.

Notice how even though this passage is talking about Jesus' death on the cross, Paul's focus is on the way it displayed the righteousness of God. He speaks of God *putting forward* Jesus as a *propitiation*. This means God offered up Jesus to stand in our place and to take the punishment we deserved—the punishment of God's own wrath. Just as He did with Abraham and Isaac on Mount Moriah, God provided His own substitute sacrifice.

Paul says He did it to demonstrate His own righteousness 'because in his divine forbearance he had passed over former sins' (v. 25). What does this mean? Paul is teaching us that God felt the need to defend His righteousness or His justice (see the NIV) because of the sins of those who came before Jesus Christ. Have you ever wondered how Old Testament saints like Abraham, Moses, Job, or Daniel were saved? Was it by law-keeping and good works? That is impossible because we know that 'by works of the law no one will be justified' (Gal. 2:16), and that 'it is impossible for the blood of bulls and goats to take away sins' (Heb. 10:4). So how were Old Testament believers saved if their sins were not truly taken away? It is only possible because of the cross and the forbearance, or foreknowledge, of God. You see, in the times of Abraham or Moses or Daniel, God knew that one day Jesus would suffer God's wrath for the sins of the world. So, God temporarily passed over those sins. He did not ignore them or sweep them under the rug. He essentially wrote Himself an I.O.U. until that fateful day when Jesus hung upon the cross. When the time had come, Jesus suffered, not only for the sins of those who would come after, but also for the sins of those who came before.

God knew, if He passed over sins, some might see that as unjust. The blood of bulls and goats does not take away sins, and yet Old Testament believers could be saved? That's not right! God is not following through on His Word! But the cross vindicates God. It shows the world He is indeed just. He saves people, not by ignoring their sin, but by punishing it in a sinless, undeserving substitute— His own Son. This is what Paul means when he says, 'so that he might be *just and the justifier* of the one who has faith in Jesus' (v. 26). This is how God can both punish sins and forgive sinners. This is how He can remain just while justifying those who have broken His law. The cross not only shows us the glory and love of Jesus, but also the glory and love of God the Father.

Transformed not Destroyed

When Moses asked to see God's glory on Mount Sinai in Exodus 33, God told him that if any human saw the fullness of His glory it would destroy them. No one may see God and live. So when God blessed Israel by making His presence dwell in the Tabernacle's Most Holy Place, and later the temple, they placed a curtain on the outside to separate God's presence from the place where the priests ministered, so that no one would catch an accidental, life-ending glimpse of God's glory. People understand this principle intuitively, which is why the immediate and instinctual reaction of people who think they have seen God is to fall down on their faces. Avert your eyes! Your life depends on it.

But the good news of the gospel is that the coming of Jesus has changed the way we relate to God. Again, let us turn to the words of John: 'Beloved, we are God's children now, and what we will be has not yet appeared; but we know that when he appears we shall be like him, because we shall see him as he is' (1 John 3:2).

First, note that when Jesus returns, we will see Him as He is. What does this mean? It means Jesus will show Himself to the world in all His glory. His first coming was humble and accompanied with little fanfare. His glory was hidden. 'He had no form or majesty that we should look at him, and no beauty that we should desire him' (Is. 53:2). But when He comes again every eye will see Him and all will know He is the glorious, all-powerful, conquering king who has returned to crush His enemies and rescue those who are His.

Note also what will happen to us. John says we shall be like Him *because* we shall see Him as He is. Our bodies will be transformed to be like His glorious body (Phil. 3:21) *as a result* of seeing Him in His glorified state. The sight of Him will cause a transformation in us. And so, when Jesus comes, instead of the sight of God destroying us, this sight of God—God the Son—will transform us. I have often said the story of the Bible is an answer to the question, *How can sinners dwell in the presence of a holy God without being destroyed?* The answer is always Jesus.

So let us fix our eyes on Jesus (Heb. 12:2). Let us long for His appearing (2 Tim. 4:8). Let us be like the Greeks who came to Philip in John 12 and said, 'Sir, we wish to see Jesus' (John 12:21). Because when we see Jesus, we see God. 'Whoever sees me, sees him who sent me' (John 12:45).

Chapter 5

Seeing God in one another

I don't want to brag but… I sometimes get mistaken for God. It's true. Perhaps it's a certain way that I carry myself, or my extraordinary holiness, or maybe my imposing presence. Admittedly, it's just one narrow demographic of people who tend to think I'm God every now and then: *toddlers*. See, I'm a preacher, and sometimes when I preach, a three-year-old will tell their parents that God is speaking up there behind that pulpit. The beautiful irony is, when the Scriptures are read aloud, they are exactly right. But even though someone mistaking me for God is completely ridiculous, we do in fact see Him in each and every person we encounter.

'No one has ever seen God; if we love one another, God abides in us and his love is perfected in us' (1 John 4:12). Twice in our New Testaments the Apostle John tells us that 'No one has ever seen God.' In chapter three, we examined how God, in the second of the Ten Commandments, forbids us from making images to represent Him visually. Instead, He has chosen His own images. One is His Son, Jesus, as we just saw in chapter four (see John 1:18). In this chapter, we turn to examine the second (see 1 John 4:12 above). No one has ever seen God, but we see Him in one another.

Created in God's Image

On the sixth day, God began His creation of human beings by saying, 'Let us make man in our image, after our likeness' (Gen. 1:26). Remember how I said that the word *likeness* would be an important one? We are forbidden to make any visual likeness of God, but He has chosen His own. Every human being has been stamped with the image or likeness of God. Therefore, we can see God in other people, even in those who do not worship Him or acknowledge the lordship of His Son Jesus. But what does this actually mean, that we have been created in God's image?

Sometimes we will look at a young man or woman and see in them what we call the 'spitting image' of their father or mother, grandfather or grandmother. There are times when we look at them and see in their smile, or eyes, or mannerisms a loved one that has long since passed away, and it is as if a part of that loved one lives on through them. In Genesis 5, we see this passing down of the image from Adam and Eve to Seth: 'When God created man, he made him in the likeness of God. Male and female he created them, and he blessed them and named them Man when they were created. When Adam had lived 130 years, he fathered a son *in his own likeness, after his image*, and named him Seth' (Gen. 5:1-3, emphasis added). When we have children, we are imitating God's work of creating another human being in our own image, while God, on a deeper level, is creating them in His.

Human beings are unique from all of God's creation because it is only of humans that God says He created them in His image. This means we are fundamentally different from animals. No matter how close a connection some might see between, say, humans and apes, there are certain attributes God has passed on only to us. Self-consciousness, verbal language, logic, complex reasoning, wisdom, abstract thinking, morals and ethics, and the ability to suppress our instincts for the greater good are all distinguishing marks of God's image in human beings. All are, in some way, characteristics of God Himself and have been uniquely passed on to mankind alone.

We also see God's image in one another in the unique roles and tasks God has given to mankind. Genesis 1:27-28 shows us God has given us dominion over all other parts of His creation. When we exercise this dominion with wisdom and care we display the image of God who is the ultimate and perfect ruler. When

God commands Adam and Eve to 'subdue' the earth, He is not simply telling them to maintain authority over it, but to use their creativity to cultivate it. While God is the only one who can create something out of nothing, He has nevertheless given us the ability to harness the natural resources and raw materials of the earth to create something new.

One implication of this is that every human life is sacred and should be cared for and protected. Every person, regardless of age, race, gender, mental capacity, religion, etc, is an image-bearer of God. Taking the life of an image-bearer is an assault upon the image-maker Himself. In Genesis 9, as God is essentially starting over with Noah and his family, He gives them this law: 'Whoever sheds the blood of man, by man shall his blood be shed, for God made man in his own image' (Gen. 9:6).

Notice how God says that the reason it is wrong to murder someone is because God has made every person in His image. Murder is the extinguishing of one of the flames God has placed in this dark world to give off the light of His image. Ironically this is also the text that justifies the appropriate use of capital punishment. If you take the life of an image-bearer, your life could be taken from you as punishment.

This is the main reason abortion is so evil. Psalm 139:13 tells us that God is the one who does the work of forming a child in his mother's womb. There is a sense in which the parents conceive another human in their image, but it is God who ultimately creates that life. It is similar to the way the gospel spreads and takes root: 'One person plants, another waters, but it is God who gives the growth' (1 Cor. 3:7). Abortion is an act of assault on the creative work of God, and the snuffing out of another one of His image-bearers.

A second important implication of God creating us in His image is that we can see glimpses of God even in non-Christians. While God's image will be displayed most clearly in those who know Him and seek Him, unbelievers can still unwittingly exhibit God's attributes in some ways. Have you ever been blessed by the God-given talents of a non-Christian musician or artist? How many times have unbelievers made significant contributions to the good of mankind? Even our friends and family members who do not know the Lord will, display sacrificial love or contagious kindness. This is what is often called God's *common grace*, which He bestows on all of His creatures. God has created every human being in His image, believer and unbeliever, and therefore we can see God in all of them, even those who do not worship Him.

The Indwelling of God's Spirit

Yet the truth remains that we will see God most clearly in those who are His children—those who have come to Him through His Son Jesus. In Acts 2:38, after those in attendance cry out, asking what they must do to be saved, Peter replies, 'Repent and be baptized every one of you in the name of Jesus Christ for the forgiveness of your sins, and you will receive the gift of the Holy Spirit.' Notice the cause and effect language here. Those who repent and are baptized in the name of Jesus will receive the gift of the Holy Spirit. In other words, when we are baptized into Christ, with repentant faith, God sends the Holy Spirit to dwell inside of us.

From that point on, as the believer continues to walk with Christ, the Spirit works in their hearts and minds, growing them in holiness. As each week, month, or year goes by, the Spirit is making the believer more and more like Jesus. We know from places like Colossians 1 and Hebrews 1 that Jesus is the perfect image of God. As we saw in the previous chapter, we see God most clearly in Jesus. So, it follows then, that as the Spirit makes the believer more and more like Christ, we can begin to see more and more of God in that person.

Furthermore, the Holy Spirit is God's Spirit. When we are baptized in faith, God sends His own Spirit to dwell inside of us. This means every Christian is walking around with God in them! I said above that we can see glimpses of God's image even in non-Christians. This is because every human being is created in God's image, not just Christians. But we must understand that the entrance of sin into the world means God's image has been damaged in each one of us. Adam and Eve, before sin, would have exhibited the image of God in exactly the way God intended. Jesus is our only example of someone who did this for His entire life. Sin has corrupted God's image in every human being except for Jesus. However, there is good news. One of the results of the work of the Holy Spirit's indwelling presence in the life of believers is the *restoration* of the corrupted and damaged image of God within them. In Colossians 3:10, Paul speaks of the 'new self' that we put on in our baptism when the Holy Spirit comes to dwell inside of us. This new self is 'being *renewed* in knowledge after the *image* of its creator' (emphasis added).[1]

Paul also tells us that the Holy Spirit provides gifts to each believer which manifest or reveal God to others. In 1 Corinthians 12, Paul begins a three-chapters-long section on spiritual gifts, and specifically calls them 'manifestations of the Spirit for the common good' (1 Cor. 12:7). As the Spirit of God, manifestations of the Spirit are truly manifestations of God Himself in the lives of His children. So, when Christians use their gifts to serve and love one another, they are giving the rest of us a glimpse of who God is. When you use your spiritual gifts to serve your brothers and sisters in Christ, you are helping them to see God.

The Attributes of God Made Visible

In the section above on being created in God's image, one topic I deliberately did not address was the attributes of God. Theologians have traditionally divided up God's attributes into two categories: communicable and incommunicable. Communicable attributes are those that God has passed on to His image-bearers in some measure, while incommunicable attributes are those that remain absolutely unique to God—they cannot be passed on in any way. For example, only God is omniscient or all-knowing. Human beings cannot image God in this way. But there are many of God's attributes that we can experience, display, and aspire to. Take, for example, Paul's list of the fruit of the Spirit: 'But the fruit of the Spirit is love, joy, peace, patience, kindness, goodness, faithfulness, gentleness, self-control; against such things there is no law' (Gal. 5:22-23). All of these are perfectly and fully present in God, and imperfectly and partially present in those who have His Spirit dwelling inside of them.

One of the primary ways we see God in others is when they display God's attributes through their words or actions. In Numbers 25, God's anger was kindled against the men of Israel because they committed sexual immorality with the women of Moab, a surrounding nation. God tells Moses to rally the leaders that remained faithful, and put to death those Israelite men who were responsible. So, Moses meets with the faithful leaders outside the tent of meeting and tells them what must be done. As they are

---

1. See also Ephesians 4:23-24, which is almost identical to Colossians 3:10.

weeping over the sins of their brothers, and the incredibly hard task that lay before them, an astoundingly arrogant Israelite man casually strolls into the camp, arm-in-arm with a Midianite woman, and takes her into his tent. Then we read this:

> When Phinehas the son of Eleazar, son of Aaron the priest, saw it, he rose and left the congregation and took a spear in his hand and went after the man of Israel into the chamber and pierced both of them, the man of Israel and the woman through her belly. Thus the plague on the people of Israel was stopped. Nevertheless, those who died by the plague were twenty-four thousand. (Num. 25:7-9)

Twenty-four thousand Israelites had died because of the sexual immorality of these men. Yet God relented because of the righteous act of Phinehas. Does that surprise you? Does referring to Phinehas putting two people to death as a 'righteous act' cause you to bristle? Consider the way God Himself describes the incident: When God speaks to Moses about how the plague was stopped, He says, 'Phinehas the son of Eleazar, son of Aaron the priest, has turned back my wrath from the people of Israel, in that he was *jealous with my jealousy* among them, so that I did not consume the people of Israel in my jealousy' (Num. 25:10-11, emphasis added).

God says Phinehas was 'jealous with my jealousy.' Phinehas felt what God felt and acted accordingly. So, when the Israelites saw the wrath of Phinehas, they were witnessing the righteous wrath of God. This scene foreshadows Jesus' anger in the temple as He drove out the animals and the money changers. His anger was God's anger. He felt what God felt. When the people saw the anger of Jesus, they were witnessing the anger of God.

One of the ways the Spirit sanctifies us over time is He teaches us to feel what God feels—to love what God loves, but also to hate what God hates. In 1 Samuel 13:14, David was called *a man after God's own heart*. Similarly, in Jeremiah 3:15, God says, 'And I will give you shepherds after my own heart.' In other words, like Phinehas, they feel what God feels. But notice, this is not just a description of their current state. They are *after* God's own heart. It is not so much something they are as something they are becoming. They are seeking and pursuing a heart like God's. This should characterize the life of every believer. It's what this book you are reading is all about. Seeing God is all about *seeking* God, and if we find Him, and behold His glory, we will become increasingly like Him. 'And we all, with unveiled face, beholding the glory of the Lord, are being transformed into the same image from one degree of glory to another' (2 Cor. 3:18). As we become like Him more and more, others will see Him when they look at us.

Sometimes it can be hard for us to fully grasp God's love, or His patience, or His forgiveness. We read in the Bible that these things are true of Him. We have the knowledge in our heads, but how can we experience them in our hearts? This is where our brothers and sisters in Christ are so helpful. When a brother or sister is patient with us, the patience of God all of a sudden becomes concrete and tangible. In a sense, our head knowledge of God's patience moves down to our hearts. When a brother or sister forgives us, the forgiveness of God becomes more real, easier to grasp. When we are loved by a brother or sister, with a godly love, God's love moves from head knowledge to heart experience. As John said, 'No one has ever seen God; if we love one another, God abides in us and his love is perfected in us. (1 John 4:12).

The Body of Christ

Finally, we see from Scripture that the world sees God when they look at the church. We are ambassadors for the King and as a body, we represent Him to a world that has never seen Him. They can't see God, but they can see the church. What picture will we give them of the God they have never seen or known?

Jesus once said, 'In the same way, let your light shine before others, so that they may see your good works and give glory to your Father who is in heaven. (Matt 5:16). Peter, no doubt influenced by the Lord's words, similarly wrote, 'Keep your conduct among the Gentiles honorable, so that when they speak against you as evildoers, they may see your good deeds and glorify God on the day of visitation' (1 Pet. 2:12). In a culture where people are actively looking for ways to discredit the church, God is calling us to represent Him in such a way that outsiders can not help but give glory to God because of what they see.

But the greatest way we show God to the world is through the way we love one another. Again, in our theme verse for this chapter, 1 John 4:12, John emphasizes how it is our love that makes the invisible God visible. In fact, just a few verses later John writes, 'If anyone says, "I love God," and hates his brother, he is a liar; for he who does not love his brother whom he has seen cannot love God whom he has not seen' (1 John 4:20). We have never seen God, but we see one another, and if we cannot love our brothers right in front of us, how can we love the one who is unseen?

One of the clearest ways the world can see God by looking at the church is when a local church has a gospel culture. What I mean by that is a culture where the gospel is making a visible difference in the community of believers. For example, if people look at a church and see old and young, black and white, Republican and Democrat, rich and poor, all caring for one another, serving one another, and treating one another as equals, they will have no other explanation but that God has done this. Groups who cannot get along in the world, who seem like sworn enemies in today's culture, are coming together and sacrificing their own preferences and desires and possessions for the good of the other. When the world sees that kind of a culture, they will see God. There is no other possible explanation. As pastor and author Ray Ortlund says, 'The world does not believe that real unity can even exist. They have never seen it.'[2]

If our churches can be a place where the members are all convinced that Philippians 2:3 is true, we can begin to have a culture like that. There we read, 'Do nothing from selfish ambition or conceit, but in humility count others more significant than yourselves.' Do we believe that everyone else in the church is more significant, more important, than we are? If we do, we will consistently and joyfully sacrifice our preferences, our time, our money, and more for their benefit. Jesus is our ultimate example here. 'Have this mind among yourselves, which is yours in Christ Jesus, who, though he was in the form of God, did not count equality with God a thing to be grasped, but emptied himself, by taking the form of a servant, being born in the likeness of men' (Phil. 2:5-7). If Jesus Himself, being exalted above all, could voluntarily lower Himself to the place of servant of all, then our task is to consider others above ourselves. In this way, a watching world will see God in the church, and give Him glory.

---

2. Ray Ortlund, *The Gospel: How the Church Portrays the Beauty of Christ* (Wheaton: Crossway, 2014), Kindle loc. 1310.

CHAPTER 6

THE PRIMARY WAY WE SEE GOD: THE BIBLE

When I was a young boy there was no video tape in our house that got more use than our copy of *The Wizard of Oz*. One of my favorite scenes is when Dorothy, Scarecrow, Tin Man, and the Lion finally reach the front doors to the Emerald City. As the guard (one of the many characters played by Frank Morgan in one of the all-time great acting performances) answers the door, a comical conversation ensues. At one point Dorothy says, 'We want to see the Wizard!' Shocked and completely flustered, the guard replies, 'The Wizard?! But nobody can see the Great Oz! Nobody's ever seen the Great Oz. Even I've never seen him!' And then Dorothy replies, 'Well... then how do you know there is one?'

That puts us in quite a predicament, now doesn't it? No one has ever seen God. Even I've never seen Him! So then... how do we know there is one?

There are all kinds of philosophical arguments for the existence of God. There's the argument of a finely-tuned universe, the argument that for the universe to exist it had to have a cause, the existence of morality, and so on. But ultimately, for human beings to know the transcendent, infinite, and incomprehensible God, He must reveal Himself. It is the only way for us to see Him.

53

Of course, God has revealed Himself in a number of ways. Paul tells us in Romans 1 that God has created every human being in such a way that when we look out at creation, we all understand that there is a God who made all of this, and that we owe Him our allegiance. Unfortunately, as Paul goes on to tell us, now that sin has entered our world and our experience, this knowledge of God's glory is only enough to condemn us. But the good news is that God has provided us with a revelation of Himself that is much more firm and complete than creation. 'Jesus is God's ultimate revelation, but for those of us living in the twenty first century, the primary way God has revealed Himself is in His sure and complete Word, the Bible.' Since Scripture is the primary way God has revealed Himself, it is the primary way we see Him, and it must be the primary way we seek Him.

All Other Means Are Subjective

The danger of putting too much stock in other ways of seeing God, besides the Bible, is that you can misinterpret those experiences. They are subjective, whereas the Bible is objective and external to us. Granted, the Bible can also be misinterpreted, but with Scripture the words are there on the page. They are the same for you as they are for me. But with personal experience, you are the only one who can interpret or misinterpret it. When someone tells the story of their own spiritual experience, they can swat away any skepticism because, after all, how can anyone disprove what they are claiming?

When I was in college there was a noticeable hunger among the Christian students around me to hear directly from God. They longed for more than just the Bible. If God would only speak to me directly! For a time, I fell into this trap as well. I wanted nothing more than for God to give me some special message. I ached for it. As time went by, and nothing happened, I questioned my faith and my love for Him. A common practice in those days was for a fellow student to come up and give you a 'word from God.' Apparently, God had spoken to them and they were supposed to pass on to you what He said. The problem was, no one knew whether or not God had actually spoken. Maybe He did, or maybe that person was simply gullible, caught up in the emotion of it all. The worst was when someone insisted the Lord had given them a glimpse of someone else's future. It was always something special or particularly exciting that God was about to do in their lives. But when the time came, and the supposed miracle never happened, the ones on the receiving end of those words were left with a spiritual crisis. *Did I do something wrong? Do I just not have enough faith?* You can see how hurtful these kinds of things can become.

Seeking after unique words from the Lord by practices such as listening prayer opens us up to all kinds of inaccurate and murky theology, not to mention satanic deception. In 2 Corinthians 11, Paul warns us against false prophets by saying, 'And no wonder, for even Satan disguises himself as an angel of light. So, it is no surprise if his servants, also, disguise themselves as servants of righteousness. Their end will correspond to their deeds' (2 Cor. 11:14-15). This is not to say that everyone who claims to have a word from the Lord is proactively serving Satan. Many of them, no doubt, have a sincere desire to do the will of the Lord. But it does mean that in seeking out this extra-biblical revelation, they are needlessly opening themselves up to being deceived. (Not to even get into the debate over whether these gifts have ceased or not in the present day.)

The Bible is the primary way God has revealed Himself, and thus is the primary way we must seek to see Him. All other means are secondary and less certain. We do not need visions or unique words from the Lord when He has spoken clearly, definitively, and sufficiently in His Word. As Peter says, 'we have the prophetic word more fully confirmed' (2 Pet. 1:19). In that section of his second epistle, Peter had just spoken of his experience witnessing the transfiguration of Jesus, and hearing God speak audibly from heaven proclaiming His approval of His Son. But even after that majestic encounter, Peter knew the Scriptures to be much more solid and trustworthy than anyone's personal experience. Even seeing God in others, as we covered in the last chapter, is secondary to seeing Him in the Bible. You might say God's revelation of Himself in Christ is primary, but even for that, we can only see Christ through the eye-witness accounts of His life in Scripture.

The God Who Makes Himself Known

In chapter one we saw that God is a God who desires to give us Himself. He created us so that our hearts would only be satisfied in Him. But He did not simply leave us groping in the dark. Paul tells us in Acts 17:26-27 that He has created the world and ordered it so that people would seek Him and 'perhaps feel their way toward him and find him.' He wants to be found, and so He reveals Himself.

The Bible itself is God's once and for all act of self-revelation. While that word *revelation* is used for the title of the final book in the canon of Scripture, we should not think this means the rest of the Bible is something different. No, it is all revelation—God's revelation of Himself to us. This is the primary way we should think about the Bible. It is first and foremost a book written by God, telling us about Himself and how we should respond to Him.

Within the pages of Scripture we find consistent examples of God showing Himself to His people so they could know Him. It begins with His presence in the garden of Eden with Adam and Eve. It continues as He takes the initiative to speak to Cain, Abraham, Isaac, Jacob, Joseph, and many others. The ten plagues and the exodus from Egypt were a magnificent display of God's power and glory. He gives His law to Moses and the Israelites on Mount Sinai.

All of this leads to God dwelling in the midst of His people, first in the portable tabernacle, and later in the temple at Jerusalem. While His presence must be concealed and heavily mediated to protect the people, it is nonetheless an amazing act of self-giving love that God goes to such lengths to return to His people after Adam and Eve's sin drove them from His presence.

Despite the continued rebellion of His people, God eventually shows Himself in Jesus, God in the flesh. In fact, in the opening words of John's gospel account he says that the coming of Jesus meant God had taken on flesh and had come to dwell among us (John 1:14). The Greek word John uses for 'dwelt among us' here literally means 'tabernacled'—the noun for God's Old Testament dwelling place transformed into a verb! For readers of John's gospel who were familiar with this God who desires to show Himself, this word-choice by John was perfectly fitting. Jesus was the fulfillment of the tabernacle and the temple. Indeed, He was the perfect temple. 'Destroy this temple,' He told the Jews, 'and in three days I will raise it up' (John 2:19). They did not know He was referring to His own body.

As we follow the temple language throughout Scripture, we see that after Jesus' ascension, the role of temple (God's dwelling place on earth) passed on to the church (1 Cor. 3:16-17), and each individual Christian (1 Cor. 6:19). God continues to show Himself.

He continues to dwell with us. He has every right to withdraw from us; it is nothing more than our sins deserve. And yet the consistent pattern in Scripture is a God who pursues having a presence with His people.

So many today see God as a distant, strict disciplinarian who is constantly disappointed and upset with us. Some even think He is out to ruin our happiness and keep us from having fun. And while we do see His holiness, His justice, and even His wrath clearly displayed in the Bible, we also see His astonishing compassion, patience, understanding, gentleness, and generosity toward us. God is love (1 John 4:8, 16), and a God of self-giving love is radically different than what anyone would expect from an all-powerful deity who alone is ruler over the universe. Yet that is what we find when we read God's words to us about Himself.

The Importance of Deep Doctrine

There are those who, in an effort to have intimacy with God, or we might say in an effort to see more of God, avoid deep doctrine and theology. Undoubtedly, this attitude is the result of having seen a misuse of doctrine in the church. For some, the study of theology leads to a knowledge that puffs up and not a love that builds up (1 Cor. 8:1). It can produce a dryness or an arrogance that turns other believers off, as well it should. But this is not the proper end of deep doctrine and theology. Doctrine should lead us to worship. It should lead us to seeing the glory of God. And if that is the case, the more doctrine, the better.

The Bible is God's self-revelation, therefore we need to study it to accurately know this God we long to see. A verse here or there will not give us an accurate picture. Nor will studying only certain portions of the Bible while neglecting others (for example, never reading the Old Testament). Yes, God is love (1 John 4:8, 16), but that is not all He is! He is also spirit (John 4:24), light (1 John 1:5), and a consuming fire (Heb. 12:29). If we do not seek God by studying His entire self-revelation, we will misunderstand and misrepresent Him. We will have a distorted and unbalanced view of Him and thus open ourselves up to breaking the second commandment.

Jesus told the woman at the well, 'God is spirit, and those who worship him must worship in spirit and truth' (John 4:24).

To worship God in truth means to worship Him as He has revealed Himself. Doctrine not only *should* lead to worship, it *must* be what leads us to worship. Otherwise, we will be worshiping a false idea of God. To see God intensely and intimately, we don't need less doctrine. We need more! The doctrine we find in the Bible is the fuel for our worship and for seeing God. Would you rather have your feelings or circumstances as fuel? Of course not.

So, let us not allow our study of doctrine and theology lead us to a dry arrogance. But let us also not go to the other extreme and therefore avoid doctrine altogether. Let's pursue God by the means He has given us to pursue Him: His Word.

Preaching is Helping People See God

The preaching of God's Word has always been, and will always be, central to the church because the Word is where God has chosen to reveal Himself. Paul tells us, 'So faith comes from hearing, and hearing through the word of Christ' (Rom. 10:17). Preaching is quite simply the proclamation of God's Word to God's people. A church that hears the faithful preaching of God's Word, week in and week out, will learn how to see God, not with their physical eyes, but with the eyes of their hearts.

This kind of preaching requires a preacher who has done the work of seeing God for Himself. In John 12, John notes how those who saw Jesus' miracles, and still refused to believe, were actually fulfilling the words of Isaiah in the Old Testament. After quoting a few passages from Isaiah about spiritual blindness, John then writes these words: 'Isaiah said these things *because he saw his glory and spoke of him*' (John 12:41, emphasis added). The reason Isaiah could proclaim the glory of God is because he saw it for himself. Remember Isaiah's vision of the Lord in Isaiah 6? It wrecked him. It changed him. It fueled him for the rest of his life to do the hard work of proclaiming God's truth to those around him.

For preaching to help people see God, it must come from a preacher who has himself seen God. Isaiah 40:9 describes the God-appointed task of the preacher perhaps better than any other passage in Scripture: 'Go on up to a high mountain, O Zion, herald of good news; lift up your voice with strength, O Jerusalem, herald of good news; lift it up, fear not; say to the cities of Judah, "Behold your God!"' This is the essence of preaching: saying to the people, 'Behold your God!' True preaching is not motivational self-help, or dynamic vision-casting, or even angry scolding. True preaching is helping people to see and behold God!

The God of Words

It should not surprise us that God's primary chosen method of self-revelation is through words in a book. Throughout Scripture we find that this God is a God of words. His Word has long been a method by which He chooses to reveal Himself. In 1 Samuel 3:21 we read, 'And the Lord appeared again at Shiloh, for the Lord revealed himself to Samuel at Shiloh by the word of the Lord.' Did you notice that? He appeared, but He also revealed Himself *by the word of the Lord*.

Over and over again in the Old Testament, as God revealed Himself to His chosen prophets, He spoke to them. Sometimes they saw a form of Him. Sometimes they heard the voice only. But the voice was always primary. In Deuteronomy 4, Moses reminds the people that God intentionally did not show them any form of Himself when He appeared to them at Mount Sinai. They saw smoke and lightning, but they did not really see God visually at all. He spoke, first to the people, then to Moses.

When Moses was on that mountain, alone with God, and asked to see His glory, God told him, 'man shall not see me and live' (Ex. 33:20). Nevertheless, God did graciously grant Moses the opportunity to see a portion of His glory. God hid Moses in a cleft of the rock, and passed by him. How did God *show* His glory to Moses as He passed by? With words. God proclaimed His name to Moses.

> The Lord passed before him and proclaimed, 'The Lord, the Lord, a God merciful and gracious, slow to anger, and abounding in steadfast love and faithfulness, keeping steadfast love for thousands, forgiving iniquity and transgression and sin, but who will by no means clear the guilty, visiting the iniquity of the fathers on the children and the children's children, to the third and the fourth generation.' (Ex. 34:6-7)

This verbal proclamation—not any visual display—was how God answered Moses' request, 'Please, show me your glory' (Ex. 33:18). God consistently reveals Himself to His people through His words.

This makes sense when we consider the power of words versus the power of images. Images can certainly evoke strong emotions in us, and they can help us comprehend what was previously hard to imagine. But words can do so much more. The reason a book has so much more potential than its movie adaptation is not just because the author can fit in more content. It is because the story on the page leaves so much more up to the imagination of the reader, whereas a movie is essentially giving the viewer a look into one person's imagination—often the director's. My favorite book outside the Bible is *The Lord of the Rings* trilogy. Thanks to Peter Jackson's movies, Aragorn will always look and sound like Viggo Mortenson in my mind (not that I'm complaining!). When Larry McMurtry wrote *Lonesome Dove*, he probably didn't intend for his readers to think of Tommy Lee Jones and Robert Duvall every time they read about Captain Call and Gus McCrae, but that is what happens now that the mini-series was made (again, I don't mind in the least!).

Images will always fall short of the pictures words can create in our mind. Perhaps this has something to do with God forbidding us from making Him visible in the second commandment. In fact, especially pertinent for our purpose in this book, words can help us see with the eyes of our heart what would be impossible to see with our physical eyes. Tony Reinke, author and senior teacher for Desiring God Ministries, writes,

> Images do capture stunning scenes and events, but words take you by the hand down to the depths of the human soul and up to the heights of an unseen eternity. This is why what we can learn about God by looking at his visible creation (general revelation) is limited. We need his word (special revelation) to help "see" what is invisible.[1]

A Words-Centered People

Because God is a God of words, and because His once-for-all chosen means of self-revelation is the Bible, Christianity is a word-centered religion. Throughout history Christians have been on the front lines promoting and teaching literacy across the globe because God has revealed Himself in a book for us to read. Therefore, developing the skill of reading is of the utmost importance. Our worship services

---

1. Tony Reinke, *Lit! A Christian Guide to Reading Books* (Wheaton: Crossway, 2011), Kindle loc. 705.

and ministries should be determinedly word-centered because the Bible is where we find our connection to the one who gives life.

As Kevin DeYoung puts it so well: 'We make no apology for being Word-centered and words-centered. Faith comes by hearing (Rom. 10:17). That's how God designed it because that's how He has chosen to reveal Himself. Christian worship is meant to be wordy and not a breathtaking visual display.'[2]

2.   Kevin DeYoung, *The 10 Commandments* (Wheaton: Crossway, 2018), 46.

CHAPTER 7

BEAUTY, WONDER, AND MOMENTS OF TRANSCENDENCE

Have you ever experienced a moment so significant that it felt like God had just reached down and whispered, *'I'm here'*? In Acts 14:17, Paul says that God 'did not leave himself without witness.' In other words, this God who remains unseen has not hidden Himself from us completely. He has revealed Himself in a number of ways. We have already seen a few of the primary ways He has shown us Himself, but there remains what we might call His divine hints and whispers—moments when our hearts perceive Him because the ordinary has all of a sudden become extraordinary.

In God's Word we learn that God has revealed Himself to people through a number of means throughout salvation history, including: dreams, visions and theophanies (see chapter eight). While we must acknowledge that God could indeed reveal Himself to people by these methods today, it is clear that once the Bible was completed, and the canon of Scripture closed, these forms of communication trailed off, and God's Word emerged as His primary means of revelation. However, God is still revealing Himself to all human beings, even those without access to His Word, through secondary means.

God's Glory in Nature

One of these secondary ways God allows us to see Him is through the natural world He has created. David wrote, 'The heavens declare the glory of God, and the sky above proclaims his handiwork. Day to day pours out speech, and night to night reveals knowledge' (Ps. 19:1-2). In other words, when we look at the sky, the clouds, the stars, mountains, sunrises, photos of deep space, violent storms, and a number of other features of God's good creation, we can see God with the eyes of our hearts. We see His glory, His authority, and His goodness toward us. We see His love for order, beauty, diversity, and complexity.

In Romans 1, Paul tells us that every single human being, with a capable mind, can look out at creation and intuitively understand three things: (1) there is a God that made all this, (2) we owe Him praise, and (3) we owe Him thanks (see Romans 1:18-21). In fact, this is the fundamental reason why we believe that without the gospel it is impossible for anyone to be saved. Paul says the knowledge of God we have from creation is now only enough to condemn us, because no one has honored God or given thanks to Him as they knew they should. Therefore, since Pentecost, without the gospel of Jesus Christ there is no chance to be saved. This is why, since the beginning of Christianity, the church has viewed missions as urgent and essential. If we do not get the gospel to those who do not have it, they will be separated from God for all eternity.

But this is not our main focus here. At this point, I simply want to draw your attention to Paul's acknowledgement of the fact that when we look out at creation, we see the creator. God places His fingerprints all over His creation so that human beings would become aware of Him, and their need for Him, and then 'perhaps feel their way toward him and find him. Yet he is actually not far from each one of us.' (Acts 17:27)

Brother Lawrence, a seventeenth-century French monk, first came to an understanding of God's glory through nature. His conversion story is recounted in the Christian classic *The Practice of the Presence of God*:

> He told me that it had all happened one winter day, as he was looking at a barren tree. Although the tree's leaves were indeed gone, he knew that they would soon reappear, followed by blossoms and then fruit. This gave him a

profound impression of God's providence and power, which never left him. Brother Lawrence still maintains that this impression detached him entirely from the world and gave him such a great love for God that it hasn't changed in all of the forty years he has been walking with Him.[1]

The great frustration lies in the fact that these glories are there for us to see every day, all around us, if only we have the eyes to see. As C. S. Lewis once wrote, 'The real labour is to remember, to attend. In fact, to come awake. Still more, to remain awake.'[2] But I suppose that is why you are reading this book. We are all on a quest for eyes that can see the glory of God, are we not?

Recently, one of my favorite guitarists, John Mayer, appeared in a series of advertisements for Land Rover vehicles. These ads are focused on the benefits of getting unplugged and out into nature. In one of the videos, as he spends some time deep in a forest, he says, 'You hear a lot about self-care, you hear a lot about self-love, you hear a lot about people wrestling with questions to whether they matter. I don't think you can come out here and get any other message from yourself than, "Yeah you're alright... you're ok."'[3] You are so close, John Mayer! If only he could understand that this message is not coming from himself, but the creator of it all... and that the message is not *You're ok*, but rather, *I am glorious, and my glory is the only source of true satisfaction.* John Piper once wrote, 'We are all starved for the glory of God, not self. No one goes to the Grand Canyon to increase self-esteem. Why do we go? Because there is greater healing for the soul in beholding splendor than there is in beholding self.'[4]

Paul tells us in Romans 1 that it is not as though unbelievers do not comprehend the creator and His glory. Rather, it is that they do, but instead of letting that truth wash over them and affect their lives, they suppress it (Rom. 1:18). They push it down because they

1. Brother Lawrence, *The Practice of the Presence of God* (New Kensington: Whittaker House, 1982), Kindle loc. 20.

2. C. S. Lewis, *Letters to Malcolm, Chiefly on Prayer* (New York: HarperOne, 2017), Kindle loc. 1042.

3. Atlantic Re:think, 'The Atlantic & Land Rover Present: John Mayer Goes Outside,' YouTube Video, 5:56, September 8, 2020, https://www.youtube.com/watch?v=xRvsC0sqguc.

4. John Piper, *Seeing and Savoring Jesus Christ* (Wheaton: Crossway, 2004), 15.

don't want to deal with it. Dealing with God means dealing with our sin, and that is not something everyone is willing to face.

However, the more we allow the truth of God's glory to infect us, and the longer we walk with Christ, growing in holiness, the more we will see God in our every-day experiences of creation. The Spirit gradually opens our eyes to the glory of God around us, sanctifying them bit by bit, and helping them to perceive as they should. Pastor and author Steve DeWitt, in his book *Eyes Wide Open*, writes,

> To go beyond beauty to God's beauty we must perceive the reflections of God's beauty in the world around us. To perceive it, we must be looking for it. Looking for it requires a kind of spiritual discernment enabled by the Holy Spirit and empowered by our love for God.[5]

Moments of Transcendence

The morning of June 9, 1973 was one of national anticipation in the United States. The day had finally come when the world would see if Secretariat could win the Belmont Stakes and do what no horse had done since Citation in 1948—complete the Triple Crown. Yet, even with the media frenzy, the national attention, and the hopes of what seemed like the entire country, the level of anticipation was not nearly as high as it would have been if people knew what they were about to witness later that day.

Secretariat ran what can only be described as the greatest race a horse has ever, or will ever run, in the history of the sport. Sham, who had been a close competitor to Secretariat in the first two races of the Triple Crown, finished last that day, completely worn out after his jockey desperately tried to keep pace with Secretariat from the start. The distance that separated Secretariat and the second-place horse at the finish line was thirty-one lengths, an all-time record.

What has always surprised me is how emotional I become when I hear the story told, or see footage of the race. Now, you need to understand something. I have no interest in horse racing whatsoever. I think it's kind of a silly sport. I never watch the Kentucky Derby, even though I've lived in Kentucky all my life. But when I watch the documentaries of Secretariat, or see the movie, I don't just cry.

---

5. Steve DeWitt, *Eyes Wide Open: Enjoying God in Everything* (Grand Rapids: Credo House, 2012), Kindle loc. 1749.

I weep. What in the world is wrong with me?! It's a horse race, for crying out loud!

But I am not alone. Immediately following the finish that day, people in the stands and those watching on television began to realize that what they had just witnessed was more than a horse race. Pat Lynch, then Vice President of the New York Racing Association, said, 'It was really an almost supernatural experience.' Jack Whittaker of CBS Sports said, 'Everybody was speechless. And then, when it set in, people were crying.' George Plimpton, writer for *Sports Illustrated*, was also there, and remembered, 'There were these co-eds lining the rail. Now, this sounds hard to believe, but I swear, half of them were weeping as he went by.' Jack Nicklaus, the famous golfer, recounted that he was watching the race on TV, alone, in his living room, and when Secretariat came down the final stretch, he applauded, and he wept, though he could not explain why.[6]

What would make someone weep over a horse race? Or, like me, over a documentary about a horse race that happened before I was even born? I have often struggled to put it into words, and I would say I am still coming to understand it, but I think the best explanation is this: for a brief moment, they saw the hand of God. Pat Lynch actually suspected that very thing. He said of that day, 'It was like the Lord was holding the reins; Secretariat was one of His creatures, and maybe whispered to him a "GO," and that horse really went.'[7] I think that's *exactly* what happened, and that is why people wept.

In the second film of *The Lord of the Rings* series, the evil wizard Saruman is explaining to his puppet assistant Wormtongue about how many thousands it will take to mount an assault on the fortress called Helm's Deep, where the people of Rohan have taken refuge. He takes him out onto the balcony of his tall tower revealing ten-thousand orcs on the ground below, screaming and ready for battle. The sight so shocks Wormtongue that we see him shed a tear at the imposing, awe-inspiring scene below. I have always thought that tear was a brilliant filmmaking touch, whether by the actor or director.

---

6. Matt Maisel, 'Secretariat's Triple Crown – Part 2 – Belmont Stakes,' clip from ESPN SportsCentury, Secretariat, YouTube Video, 10:30, April 12, 2007, https://www.youtube.com/watch?v=k-KvaeuIIsw.

7. Ibid.

It is an insightful illustration of how we can be moved emotionally by experiences of magnitude or glory.

Have you ever experienced a moment like that? One that moved you to such overwhelming emotion—emotion that could not be explained merely in terms of what you were witnessing? Have you ever shed tears listening to an orchestra play a symphony with no words? Why would a particular combination of musical notes cause someone to cry? It doesn't make logical sense. These are what I call, for lack of better words, moments of transcendence. You might call it a sight of transcendent beauty. Some refer to the feeling as *wonder*. They are moments when we catch a glimpse of God, beyond His ordinary work in the world and in our lives, and it leaves us with what C. S. Lewis sometimes called *longing*, or at other times *joy*. He described it as 'an unsatisfied desire which is itself more desirable than any other satisfaction.'[8] Elsewhere, he wrote, 'The sweetest thing in all my life has been the longing… to find the place where all the beauty comes from.'[9]

Perhaps you can relate to Lewis's experience of this longing as one of the sweetest feelings human beings can experience. For me, much like with Lewis, ever since I first started to discover it, it has been addicting. I am constantly pursuing it, even though it is as elusive as trying to grab smoke with your hand. When I first began experiencing it (probably through certain moments in movies from what I remember), I had no idea what to call it, or even what it was, but I knew I wanted that feeling again and again. It comes when I listen to Michael Kamen's *Overture* from the film *Robin Hood: Prince of Thieves*, or when I watch the charge of the Rohirrim scene in the third *Lord of the Rings* movie, or when I see Secretariat taking the Belmont Stakes by thirty-one lengths. Are these simply the chemical reaction of my body to overwhelming stimuli? Sure, but they are also so much more than that. They are hints, whispers, or whiffs of the transcendent glory of God.

The Place Where All the Beauty Comes From

As we are moved by transcendent displays of beauty, either in nature, or art, or entertainment, we shed tears because of the overwhelming

---

8. C. S. Lewis, *Surprised by Joy: The Shape of My Early Life* (Orlando: Harcourt, 1955), 15.

9. C. S. Lewis, *Till We Have Faces: A Myth Retold* (Orlando: Harcourt, 1980), 75.

longing in our hearts to find the place where all the beauty comes from. For a brief moment we catch a whiff of God, and the scent is beyond attractive.

Yet there is a danger here. The danger is allowing our joy and satisfaction to terminate on the creation instead of looking to the creator, the source. The reason these methods of seeing God must not be considered primary is that human beings are tempted to worship these created things, and to see them as an end in themselves, rather than letting them lead us to worship God and see Him more clearly. Lewis writes:

> The books or the music in which we thought the beauty was located will betray us if we trust to them; it was not in them, it only came through them, and what came through them was longing. These things—the beauty, the memory of our own past—are good images of what we really desire; but if they are mistaken for the thing itself, they turn into dumb idols, breaking the hearts of their worshipers. For they are not the thing itself; they are only the scent of a flower we have not found, the echo of a tune we have not heard, news from a country we have never yet visited.[10]

How many men and women are destroying their lives, and having their hearts broken, because they are seeking to quench their thirst for God with created things? They fail to recognize God's creation as a pointer to Him, and instead try to find satisfaction for their longing in objects that cannot deliver it.

Steve DeWitt provides an insightful and appropriate illustration of this with the moon and the sun:

> I am reminded of the difference between the sun and the moon. If all you had ever seen was a full moon, you might think it was the sun. After all, there are great similarities. A full moon is big and bright. If you thought that was all there was, imagine what it would be like to suddenly see the sun in all its brilliance. The moon would be usurped in your evaluation by something more magnificently brilliant and beautiful. You would never look at the moon the same way again. There would still be much to enjoy about moonlight, but it would be enjoyed for what it is—a reflected light.

---

10. C. S. Lewis, *The Weight of Glory* (New York: Harper Collins, 2009), Kindle loc. 288.

Every created pleasure and beauty that we have ever enjoyed in this world is like moonlight. Void of any comparison, they seem like the best this life has to offer. But through the gospel and the Holy Spirit, we have seen the radiant glory of the Beautiful One, Christ. This changes our perspective on the pleasure of moonlight beauty.

We used to worship reflections, but through the gospel and the Holy Spirit we discern a better beauty. Until we see the beauty of Christ, we will never see the true beauty in anything else. Once we discern His glory, however, we enjoy the moonlight of created beauties all the more because they remind us of Him. In fact, now we enjoy the moon because we love the sun. Jesus is the person we love. The created world is the reflection. If we love Him, we will love every resemblance of Him and see everything good and true in the universe as a picture of Him. The universe is all about Him, and Christians have the joy of seeing Him in all the created wonders in this world. This is a Spirit-enabled perspective that turns wonder's sensory experience of beauty into an occasion for joy, reflection, and worship.[11]

In our pursuit to see God, we can and should see Him all around us, every day. His glory is displayed in His creation in a million different ways. Our hearts perceive Him in moments of transcendence. But let us also remember that these methods of seeing God are secondary to the primary way He has revealed Himself to us: His Word. We must keep first things first, and second things second. Only then will we avoid the dangerous possibility of secondary things drawing us away from what is primary.

---

11. DeWitt, *Eyes Wide Open*, Kindle loc. 1660

Chapter 8

What happens when you see God?

You might look at the title of this chapter, think back to chapter two, and reply, 'You die, of course.' That's true, but it's not the entire story. As we have already seen, even though human beings cannot see God in His full glory and live to tell about it, God nevertheless appears to people in Scripture from time to time in a lesser or veiled form. This is what is known as a *theophany*. A theophany is simply when God manifests Himself in visual form to one or more human beings in a way that will not destroy them.

If we look at each example of this in the Bible, we begin to see patterns that tell us what generally happens when someone sees God. While the seeing we are focusing on in this book is not physical but spiritual, the natural reactions of those who saw a form of God with their physical eyes reveal what will happen to us when we see God with the eyes of our heart.

You Are Afraid

The first and most common reaction to seeing God in the Bible is fear. In Genesis 28 God appears to Jacob in a dream and speaks to him. Then we read, 'Jacob awoke from his sleep and said, "Surely the Lord is in this place, and I did not know it." And he was afraid and said, "How awesome is this place! This is none other than the house of God, and this is the gate of heaven'" (Gen. 28:16-17). Or take Moses' first encounter with God via the burning bush. After God told Moses who He is, 'Moses hid his face, for he was afraid to look at God' (Ex. 3:6).

One of the central theophanies in the Old Testament is when God brought the Isrealites out of Egyptian slavery, across the Red Sea, and to the foot of Mount Sinai:

> On the morning of the third day there were thunders and lightnings and a thick cloud on the mountain and a very loud trumpet blast, so that all the people in the camp trembled. Then Moses brought the people out of the camp to meet God, and they took their stand at the foot of the mountain. Now Mount Sinai was wrapped in smoke because the Lord had descended on it in fire. The smoke of it went up like the smoke of a kiln, and the whole mountain trembled greatly. And as the sound of the trumpet grew louder and louder, Moses spoke, and God answered him in thunder. The Lord came down on Mount Sinai, to the top of the mountain. And the Lord called Moses to the top of the mountain, and Moses went up. (Ex. 19:16-20)

This theophany is central to the story of Scripture because this is when God first gives the Israelites His law, including the Ten Commandments, as well as detailed instructions for the tabernacle and how they were to arrange their camp. It is also when Moses intercedes for the people and asks to see God's glory. The Israelites camped at the foot of Mount Sinai for almost a full calendar year before God led them out toward the Promised Land. It takes up the latter half of Exodus, the entire book of Leviticus, and the first third or so of the book of Numbers.

As the people saw this awesome manifestation of the Lord on the mountain, they were rightfully afraid.

> Now when all the people saw the thunder and the flashes of lightning and the sound of the trumpet and the mountain smoking, the people were afraid and trembled, and they stood far off and said to Moses, "You speak to us, and we will listen; but do not let God speak to us, lest we die.'" (Ex. 20:18-19)

Fear is a natural reaction to seeing God because our sinfulness and God's holiness do not mix. We know this intuitively. We all understand that if God appeared to us in full holiness, unmediated in any way, we would die. This fear is fitting and proper. Proverbs tells us, 'The fear of the Lord is the beginning of wisdom' (Prov. 1:7, 9:10). You cannot begin to go down the road to salvation and knowing God without a healthy fear of Him. Yes, this fear includes awe and reverence, but it also includes a trembling at what the Lord is capable of doing to His enemies. We should shudder at what would happen to us if we are not made right with God!

It also points us to our need for a mediator. Knowing God and being reconciled to Him is the pinnacle of true wisdom. Therefore, it makes sense that the beginning of that wisdom is a proper fear of God that drives us to the one mediator between God and man: Jesus Christ (1 Tim. 2:5). The recent push in some Christian circles to deny the wrath of God actually weakens the gospel and weakens the loving sacrifice of Christ because without God's wrath there is nothing dreadful we need to be saved from! Without God's wrath, Jesus' suffering on the cross was physical only. But a healthy, biblical view of God's wrath drives us to Jesus, the only one who can turn it away from us.

Fear is the first and proper response to seeing God, both for physical and spiritual sight. We see it in Jacob, Moses, and the Israelites. We see it in Isaiah, who upon seeing the Lord cried, 'Woe is me! For I am lost; for I am a man of unclean lips, and I dwell in the midst of a people of unclean lips; for my eyes have seen the King, the Lord of hosts!' (Is. 6:5). We see it in Daniel, who was anxious, alarmed, and said his 'color changed' when he saw the Lord (Dan. 7:15, 28).

You Fall Down in Humility

Related to fear, the second most common reaction from those who encounter the Lord is falling down in humility. Think of Peter, James, and John falling on their faces when Jesus was transfigured before them and God spoke from heaven. In fact, Scripture often uses those exact words of someone falling on their face. Abraham in Genesis 17 and 18, Balaam in Numbers 22, Joshua in Joshua 5, Ezekiel in Ezekiel 1, Daniel in Daniel 8, and John in Revelation 1 all fell on their faces in humility when they encountered God. All the Israelites, as one, fell on their faces when God's glory filled the tabernacle in Leviticus 9, and later the temple in 2 Chronicles 7.

When God appeared to Job and spoke out of a whirlwind, it humbled Job completely. The only words he could muster up in response were words of humble contrition: 'Behold, I am of small account; what shall I answer you? I lay my hand on my mouth. I have spoken once, and I will not answer; twice, but I will proceed no further' (Job 40:4-5). 'I had heard of you by the hearing of the ear, but now my eye sees you; therefore I despise myself, and repent in dust and ashes' (Job 42:5-6).

Paul's conversion began with a blinding vision of the Lord Jesus on the road to Damascus that caused Paul to immediately fall to the ground (Acts 9:4). And when Peter first saw the glory of Jesus after the miraculous catch, he fell down at the feet of Jesus and said, 'Depart from me, for I am a sinful man, O Lord' (Luke 5:8). Much like Isaiah, the sight of the glory of the Lord immediately made Peter aware of his sin, and in humility he did not consider himself worthy to be in the presence of such holiness. Peter's instincts were good, but Jesus said to him, 'Do not be afraid; from now on you will be catching men' (Luke 5:10). No wonder he left everything to follow Him. That's how it is with Jesus. The glory of God initially makes us cower in fear and humility, and rightfully so. But on the cross Jesus took our sin and our penalty so that we may now approach the throne of grace with confidence (Heb. 4:14-16)!

Seeing God produces humility in us on multiple levels. First, it causes us to see ourselves rightly. All of us understand from personal experience, when we are not looking at God, we drift toward a prideful, self-exalting view of ourselves. But when we encounter the living God, we are immediately put in our place, are we not? It is impossible to think too highly of yourself when you are staring at the majestic glory of the creator and king of the universe!

Old Testament scholar Peter Craigie, commenting on the people of Israel's encounter with God at Mount Sinai, says,

> It was the exceptional occurrence that terrified the people and reminded them of their *mortality*. It is easy to have too small a view of God in the mind, but the experience of the

presence of God may shatter the inadequacy of such a view and impress rather the awesomeness of *the living God*.[1]

So, in one sense, when we look at God we see ourselves rightly. But in another sense, when we see God and His glory it helps us take our eyes off of ourselves, which is something we desperately need in our day. I am no psychiatrist, but I think it is fairly obvious that our current culture has turned us inward to our own detriment. The issues we seek treatment for most often seem to be things like anxiety, depression, self-esteem, suicidal thoughts, and the like. The common denominator in all of these is they are *introspective* afflictions. We have become consumed with ourselves. What we need is not self-help, but a self-eclipsing view of God and His glory.[2] 'He must become greater; I must become less' (John 3:30).

Michael Reeves, author and president of Union School of Theology, in his excellent book on the fear of the Lord, writes:

> In fact, contemplating the splendor of God and so stoking our fearful wonder at him is at the heart of Christian health. 'And we all, with unveiled face, beholding the glory of the Lord, are being transformed into the same image from one degree of glory to another' (2 Corinthians 3:18). The grandeur of God pulls our focus up and away from ourselves. We wonder at a being greater than us. We therefore diminish. His magnificence distracts us and woos us from our daily self-obsession.[3]

Humility comes not only from seeing God's holiness and transcendence, but also from looking long and hard at His grace. Our deepest and most needed humility comes from marveling at God's glorious grace shown particularly in giving His only Son to die for us on the cross. Meditating on what God has done for us in the gospel should cause us to stop and wonder that He would do such a thing for a sinner like me. The fact that God sees the darkest corners of my heart, and the most embarrassing and rebellious thoughts I've ever had, and still loves me enough to punish His own

---

1. Peter Craigie, *The Book of Deuteronomy*, The New International Commentary on the Old Testament (Grand Rapids: Eerdmans, 1976), 165.

2. By this I do not mean to oppose the important work of biblical counselors and others who labor to help those in distress.

3. Michael Reeves, *Rejoice & Tremble: The Surprising Good News of the Fear of the Lord* (Wheaton: Crossway, 2021), 67.

Son for those sins, should melt my heart. The sight of God and His glorious grace in the gospel should not only produce a face-down posture, but a face wet with tears flowing from a grateful heart.

The Commander of God's Army and the Angel of the Lord

Let's take a closer look at Joshua's encounter in Joshua 5:

> When Joshua was by Jericho, he lifted up his eyes and looked, and behold, a man was standing before him with his drawn sword in his hand. And Joshua went to him and said to him, 'Are you for us, or for our adversaries?' And he said, 'No; but I am the commander of the army of the Lord. Now I have come.' And Joshua fell on his face to the earth and worshiped and said to him, 'What does my lord say to his servant?' And the commander of the Lord's army said to Joshua, 'Take off your sandals from your feet, for the place where you are standing is holy.' And Joshua did so. (Josh. 5:13-15)

Now, initially this might not seem like an encounter with God at all. The text says this is a man who calls himself the commander of the Lord's army. But notice the conversation and Joshua's response. First Joshua asks the man if He is for Israel or for their adversaries. The man's response? 'No.' Ha! It's almost as if He is saying, 'Um… wrong question.' The real question is are Joshua and the Israelites on *His* side?

But more importantly, notice how Joshua fell on his face and worshiped the man. Now, if this were a mere angel, we know what would happen next, because we have John's encounter with the angel in Revelation 19:10: 'Then I fell down at his feet to worship him, but he said to me, "You must not do that! I am a fellow servant with you and your brothers who hold to the testimony of Jesus. Worship God."' Angels refuse to accept worship that belongs exclusively to God. So, this is no angel, nor can it be a mere man. The only possible explanation is this is a theophany, God Himself appearing to Joshua as a man. This is why He tells Joshua to take off his sandals. God's presence makes the ground holy. God said the same to Moses, if you recall, from the burning bush (Ex. 3:5).

This commander of the Lord's army is similar in many ways to the mysterious 'Angel of the Lord' character that features so prominently in the book of Judges and makes other periodic appearances in the Old Testament. In Genesis 16, this Angel of the Lord appears to Hagar in the wilderness and she is convinced she has seen God Himself. Of course, she could have been mistaken, but this character continues to turn up, and His interactions as well as descriptions of Him keep suggesting He is more than your typical angel. In Judges 2, for instance, the Angel shows up and tells the people:

> I brought you up from Egypt and brought you into the land that I swore to give to your fathers. I said, 'I will never break my covenant with you, and you shall make no covenant with the inhabitants of this land; you shall break down their altars.' But you have not obeyed my voice. What is this you have done? So now I say, I will not drive them out before you, but they shall become thorns in your sides, and their gods shall be a snare to you. (Judg. 2:1-3)

Notice, He does not say it was God (as in, someone else) who did this. He uses the first person. He was the one who did it. As we saw in chapter two, Gideon encounters this figure in Judges 6 and fears for his life because he is convinced he has seen God. The text tells us the Lord Himself comforted Gideon, and Gideon built an altar there to the Lord. The text uses God's name (YAHWEH) and the Angel of the Lord interchangeably.

You Worship

The third most common reaction by those who see God in Scripture is worship. I suppose you could call the first two reactions we looked at above worship, but for the sake of clarity I have separated this out into its own category. Particularly, there are a number of times in the Old Testament when an encounter with God led someone to build an altar at the place God appeared and to worship Him there. Take Abram in Genesis 12, for example:

> Then the Lord appeared to Abram and said, 'To your offspring I will give this land.' So, he built there an altar to the Lord, who had appeared to him. From there he moved to the hill country on the east of Bethel and pitched his tent, with Bethel on the west and Ai on the east. And there he built an altar to the Lord and called upon the name of the Lord. (Gen. 12:7-8)

The biblical phrase, found here in verse 8, 'called upon the name of the Lord,' makes for an interesting study. It first appears in Genesis 4: 'To Seth also a son was born, and he called his name Enosh. At that time people began to call upon the name of the Lord' (Gen. 4:26). It likely means worship or prayer, or perhaps both simultaneously.[4] We see the same pattern from Abraham's son Isaac in Genesis 26:24-25—he encounters God, builds an altar, and then calls upon the name of the Lord. Gideon also built an altar after his encounter with God in Judges 6.

King Nebuchadnezzar worshiped God after two specific and powerful encounters: the fiery furnace in Daniel 3, and his own humiliation at God's hands in Daniel 4. We see later, in the book of Daniel, that Nebuchadnezzar's worship of God was not fully informed, nor did it seem to make a lasting difference in his life, but it did seem to be a form of true worship in the moment.

A final example would be the centurion stationed at the cross where Jesus died. 'And when the centurion, who stood facing him, saw that in this way he breathed his last, he said, "Truly this man was the Son of God!"' (Mark 15:39). He saw God the Son, and the beautiful humility and courage He showed in His manner of death, and he worshiped. Yet again we find that the cross provides us with perhaps the greatest and most glorious sight of God. Worship is the only proper response!

Others Will Notice

> When Moses came down from Mount Sinai, with the two tablets of the testimony in his hand as he came down from the mountain, Moses did not know that the skin of his face shone because he had been talking with God. Aaron and all the people of Israel saw Moses, and behold, the skin of his face shone, and they were afraid to come near him. (Exodus 34:29-30)

Moses had just spent significant time in the presence of the Lord on Mount Sinai. When he came down from the mountain, people could tell he had been with God. He had to put a veil over his face, it was shining so brightly. The text tells us, after that, when Moses

---

4. For a book-length treatment of this phrase see J. Gary Millar, *Calling on the Name of the Lord: A Biblical Theology of Prayer.* New Studies in Biblical Theology. (Grand Rapids: IVP Academic, 2016).

would go into the tent of meeting to talk with the Lord, his face would once again be shining when he came out, and he would have to put the veil on again until it wore off.

When you have seen God, when you have spent time with Him, people notice. God shines through. Often, like Moses, you will not even be aware of it. But others will. They will stop and take note, just like the Jewish rulers, elders, and scribes in Acts 4: 'Now when they saw the boldness of Peter and John, and perceived that they were uneducated, common men, they were astonished. And they recognized that they had been with Jesus' (Acts 4:13). If you spend a little time every day pursuing God through prayer, Bible reading, and meditation, people will recognize that you have been with God. It sounds so simple… and it is! There is no esoteric secret formula to becoming someone that others recognize as having been with God. You just need to consistently go be with Him.

Think of the times when you have seen this in others. I think of my friend Dave. Every time we speak, he exudes the humility, peace, joy, and the fervent spirit of someone who has spent time with the Lord. Our conversations never fail to turn to spiritual things. When I was in college, and I was beginning to discern a call on my life to preach God's Word, I was attracted to the preaching of John Piper. Sure, he was a dynamic speaker with great knowledge of the Scriptures, but for me it was something in his speech and manner that made it clear he had been with God. It was almost a glow, just like Moses. And I have rarely felt it more strongly than when I read A. W. Tozer's classic *The Pursuit of God*. It jumps off the page at you. This man clearly and unmistakably spent plenty of time in intimate communion with God.

As you seek and behold God, others will not fail to notice, not only because His glory rubs off on you, but because you will begin to tell others about it. This is another one of those natural reactions to seeing God. When we see a thrilling end to a sporting event, or a surprisingly good movie, we tell people about it. New parents and grandparents cannot help but show off pictures of their little ones. It is our nature to share our joy and awe with others. It follows then, that when we behold the one thing in all the universe that produces the most joy and inspires the greatest awe, we will tell others about Him. Once again, we find Peter and John as wonderful examples:

So, they called them and charged them not to speak or teach at all in the name of Jesus. But Peter and John answered them, 'Whether it is right in the sight of God to listen to you rather than to God, you must judge, for we cannot but speak of what we have seen and heard.' (Acts 4:18-20)

You Are Transformed

One of the consistent themes of the Bible is *we become what we behold*. In other words, what we constantly fix our gaze on, what we admire, what we devote our hearts to, that is what we slowly become. This principle shows up in numerous places in Scripture. For example, in the Psalms we read, in regard to idols, 'Those who make them become like them; so do all who trust in them' (Psalm 115:8, 135:18). In Isaiah 6:10 God curses His people with a dullness that intentionally mirrors their idols. In 2 Kings 17:15 we read, 'They went after false idols and became false.' We become what we behold.

The negative side of the lesson is this: don't spend time beholding anything less than God. But on the positive side, this principle teaches us that if we spend time beholding God, we will become like Him. A godly life full of godly love and service and wisdom and holiness springs forth from a heart that is continually beholding God Himself. Paul tells us, 'And we all, with unveiled face, beholding the glory of the Lord, are being transformed into the same image from one degree of glory to another' (2 Cor. 3:18).

So, we are pursuing the sight of God because we know that if we can see (or behold) Him, we will rightly fear Him. The sight of His glory and grace will humble us and take our eyes off of ourselves. We will naturally respond with worship as our joy and awe overflow into praise. We will come away shining and speaking in such a way that others will take note we have been with God. And, perhaps most importantly, if we can behold God, we will be transformed, or, you might say, be conformed to His image, little by little, from one degree of glory to another.

Chapter 9

Spiritual blindness

A blind man knows he is blind. He comprehends that others can see while he cannot. The unique thing about spiritual blindness, however, is that the spiritually blind person does not know he is blind. He believes he can see just fine. Consider the story of the man born blind in John 9. The entire chapter is a lesson in spiritual blindness. Jesus heals the man of his physical blindness, showcasing God's power over the physical effects of sin, but when the man is brought before the Pharisees, they refuse to accept that he has been healed. They even bring his parents in for questioning. Later, Jesus gives them a lesson in spiritual blindness:

> Jesus said, 'For judgment I came into this world, that those who do not see may see, and those who see may become blind.' Some of the Pharisees near him heard these things, and said to him, 'Are we also blind?' Jesus said to them, 'If you were blind, you would have no guilt; but now that you say, "We see," your guilt remains.' (John 9:39-41)

They claimed to have the power of spiritual sight in and of themselves, without Jesus. They did not need God to open their eyes. To suggest anything of the sort was an insult to them. Ironically, the man born blind had more spiritual sight than the Pharisees whose physical eyes were healthy. As Jesus explains to the disciples, the Pharisees are examples of those who 'seeing they do not see' (Matt.13:13). They could not see the glory of God, even when it was standing right in front of them.

If we long to see God, it would be helpful to pause and think about what could prevent us from seeing Him. We can only see God with spiritual sight, with the eyes of our hearts. Therefore, we must know all we can about spiritual blindness, and God's Word has much to say on it. Let's look at some of the primary causes for spiritual blindness that we find in Scripture.

Loving the World

'Do not love the world or the things in the world. If anyone loves the world, the love of the Father is not in him.' (1 John 2:15) The first barrier to spiritual sight is when we love the world or the things of the world. Just as Jesus said we cannot serve two masters (Matt. 6:24), so also we cannot gaze at two different objects, especially when they are opposed to one another. This love of the world can manifest itself in a number of ways. A love of money and the possessions or power it can buy will lead you into all kinds of evils, and has led many away from the faith (1 Tim. 6:9-10). The rich young man had a chance to follow Jesus. If he had, like the Apostles, he would have been privileged to see God like few others. Yet, when the moment of decision came, he walked away sad because he desired wealth more than God (Matt.19:16-22). He was blinded by the world.

Another manifestation of love for the world is a desire for the praise of men. Jesus once asked the Pharisees, 'How can you believe, when you receive glory from one another and do not seek the glory that comes from the only God?' (John 5:44). This came immediately after He told them they had never heard or *seen* God (John 5:37). Living for the praise of others makes seeing God impossible. Scripture tells us only those with pure and humble hearts will see God (Ps. 24:4). To come to God, we must die to ourselves and to the world. These are impossible for someone living for the praise of the world. Do you long to see God or to be seen by others? Let king Herod be a warning to us:

> On an appointed day Herod put on his royal robes, took his seat upon the throne, and delivered an oration to them. And

the people were shouting, 'The voice of a god, and not of a man!' Immediately an angel of the Lord struck him down, because he did not give God the glory, and he was eaten by worms and breathed his last. (Acts 12:21-23)

Loving Your Sin

The second barrier to seeing God is cherishing sin. In John 3, as Jesus is talking with Nicodemus, He tells him:

> And this is the judgment: the light has come into the world, and people loved the darkness rather than the light because their works were evil. For everyone who does wicked things hates the light and does not come to the light, lest his works should be exposed. But whoever does what is true comes to the light, so that it may be clearly seen that his works have been carried out in God. (John 3:19-21)

We will talk more about the biblical theme of *light* in a later chapter. For now, I want you to notice what Jesus says is the true reason why people do not come to the light that opens the eyes of their hearts. People did not reject Jesus because of a lack of evidence, or because He was not compelling. They rejected Him because they *loved* the darkness. And why did they love the darkness? Because their own works were evil. They did not want them exposed. In other words, they loved their sin. When people love their sin, they want to remain in the dark. They would not put it this way, but they would rather remain blind. It's a form of the 'ignorance is bliss' way of life.

The author and apologist, Hugh Ross, in his book *The Creator and the Cosmos*, presents a wealth of scientific evidence for belief in a creator. It is a fascinating read that will strengthen your faith and confidence. Toward the end of the book he recounts speaking at a prestigious American university where he presented his evidence to a group of science professors. After the talk, four physics professors told Ross how they could not deny the truth of his message that day. He asked them if they could see, then, the rationality of turning over their lives to Jesus Christ. They responded by saying, yes, they could see it, but they were not yet ready to be that rational. Why not? In a moment of admirable honesty, one of the professors admitted he was not ready to give up sexual immorality.[1]

---

1. Hugh Ross, *The Creator and the Cosmos* (Colorado Springs: NavPress, 2001), 217.

He saw the rationale, but not the glory or the beauty of Christ. His sin blinded him to seeing the value of the treasure that is worth selling all you have to get (Matt. 13:44). It was not a lack of knowledge or evidence. The issue was in this man's heart. He *preferred* the darkness to the light because he loved his sin. In 2 Thessalonians 2:10, Paul says of those who are perishing, 'They refused to love the truth and so be saved.' It was not that they didn't know the truth, but that they didn't *love* it. They did not cherish it above everything else. We must forsake our sin to follow Jesus. We must trade in a lesser, fleeting pleasure for a greater, more lasting one.

Paul also speaks of this in Ephesians 4: 'Now this I say and testify in the Lord, that you must no longer walk as the Gentiles do, in the futility of their minds. They are darkened in their understanding, alienated from the life of God because of the ignorance that is in them, due to their hardness of heart' (Eph. 4:17-18). Notice how he says they are alienated from God because of their ignorance, but their ignorance is a result of *their hardness of heart*. This, again, is a willful blindness due to a consistent pattern of rejecting God. The book of Hebrews tells us that the deceitfulness of sin can harden our hearts (Heb. 3:13). Sin promises satisfaction and ultimately delivers disappointment, pain, and suffering. Satan's game is not truth in advertising.

Satan Has Blinded Unbelievers

We must understand that Satan always plays a role in spiritual blindness. 2 Corinthians 4:4 speaks of those who are perishing and says, 'In their case the god of this world has blinded the minds of the unbelievers, to keep them from seeing the light of the gospel of the glory of Christ, who is the image of God.' His goal is to keep us from seeing the glory of Christ in the gospel. He knows that once we see it we are lost to him. So, he will do everything in his power to keep people in the dark.

For some, this means he works to prevent them from hearing the gospel altogether. This is why missions and evangelism are so important. If they never hear the gospel, they cannot be saved. So, we must take it to them (see Romans 1:18-21 and 10:14-17). For Christians in America this has historically meant reaching the unreached people groups of third-world countries. However, in recent years the secularization of America and other 'progressive' nations means that a number of children grow up in homes and atmospheres now where the gospel is never mentioned. Do you realize that in a generation there will be tens of thousands of *American adults* who will have never actually heard the gospel?

For others, Satan utilizes his main method of attack: deception. Jesus tells us, 'He was a murderer from the beginning, and does not stand in the truth, because there is no truth in him. When he lies, he speaks out of his own character, for he is a liar and the father of lies' (John 8:44). From the very beginning he has been trying to influence people to doubt God's goodness, His trustworthiness, and His wisdom (see Genesis 3:1-5). If he can deceive people into believing the lie that sin is better than Jesus, or that the gospel is foolishness, he can keep them in the dark.

Does God Cause Spiritual Blindness?

It might surprise you to learn that sometimes God causes a person to be spiritually blind. At first this may seem wrong and set off your spiritual red flags. Why would God ever want to prevent someone from seeing Him? But a closer look at our Bibles will reveal numerous times where God hides Himself or draws back from people due to their sin or hardness of heart. You will even find that sometimes God actively causes people to be spiritually blind as a judgment for hardening their hearts and resisting Him.

We just looked at 2 Thessalonians 2:10 above. The very next two verses say, 'Therefore God sends them a strong delusion, so that they may believe what is false, in order that all may be condemned who did not believe the truth but had pleasure in unrighteousness' (2 Thess. 2:11-12). In other words, there may come a point where someone has refused Christ—refused to love the truth—for so long that God does something to confirm them in their stiff-necked unbelief. To use the language of Paul in Romans 1, He 'gives them up' to their sinful desires. You might say He gives them what they want. Theologians call this God's *passive wrath*, which means instead of sending suffering, He removes His protective hand and lets them stumble into self-destruction. An Old Testament example comes from Ezekiel 16:42, where God tells the Israelites, 'My jealousy shall depart from you. I will be calm and will no more be angry.' At first glance, this may seem encouraging. God will no longer be angry with them! But it is far from encouraging. Indeed, this is one of the most frightening statements of God's judgment in the entire Bible. He is saying He will withdraw His care and concern for them altogether. He will allow them to destroy themselves in their lust for sin. God's passive wrath is a horrible thing to imagine.

In Romans 11:7-12, Paul talks about God's hardening of the Israelites for a time so that more Gentiles would come to know Christ and be saved. Once again, this hardening is a response to the Israelites having hardened themselves against God's revelation in Christ. Also, this text shows us that this hardening is not final. It does not seal their eternal fate. It is not beyond recovery (see verse 11). But you cannot escape the clear language that this hardening comes directly from God. He is actively causing their spiritual blindness, at least for a time. This seems also to be the nature of God's judgment upon the Israelites, which He commissioned Isaiah to go and proclaim to them in Isaiah 6:

> And he said, 'Go, and say to this people: "Keep on hearing, but do not understand; keep on seeing, but do not perceive." Make the heart of this people dull, and their ears heavy, and blind their eyes; lest they see with their eyes, and hear with their ears, and understand with their hearts, and turn and be healed.' (Is. 6:9-10)

So yes, God causes spiritual blindness. It is a judgment upon those who have hardened their hearts against Him and stubbornly refused to love the truth and so be saved. They have closed their eyes and their hearts against God for so long that He confirms them in their blindness. He withdraws His light-giving power and gives them what they want.

Bible Knowledge Alone Is Not Enough

We have seen that the Bible is God's primary means of revealing Himself to mankind. It is the primary way He shines His light into our hearts to give us the knowledge that leads to spiritual sight (2 Cor. 4:6). Nevertheless, there is a warning in our New Testaments that we cannot miss, and that we must heed. Bible knowledge alone does not guarantee spiritual sight.

The angry, legalistic preacher who clearly does not know the love and compassion of Christ. The man who fancies himself the online doctrine police, ravenously hunting for another heretical Facebook post to slam. The New Testament scholar who increasingly denies the historical reliability of the gospels. Each one has a knowledge of the Bible and yet seemingly remains spiritually blind. We have all likely encountered someone who served as a prime example of this biblical warning. In Jesus' day it was the Pharisees, the expert teachers of the Old Testament Scriptures.

Jesus said to the Pharisees in John 5, 'You search the Scriptures because you think that in them you have eternal life; and it is they that bear witness about me, yet you refuse to come to me that you may have life' (John 5:39-40). They knew their Old Testaments like the back of their hand, but when the one whom all the Scriptures pointed to showed up in their midst, they couldn't recognize Him. It was literally true of them: they wouldn't recognize God if He was right in front of their faces. Take the chief priests and the scribes in Matthew 2 as another example. They could discern from the Old Testament Scriptures where the Christ was to be born, but they did not go worship Him.

If these experts in the Scriptures missed the point of it all, how can we make sure we do not fall to the same blindness? We must be born again. Jesus said, 'Unless one is born again he cannot *see* the kingdom of God' (John 3:3, emphasis added). There is no spiritual sight without spiritual birth. We must be born of water and the Spirit (John 3:5). We must repent of our sins, confess Jesus as Lord, and be baptized into His death. Only God can cure spiritual blindness. He must speak His words of power, 'Let there be light!' in our hearts (2 Cor. 4:6). He has promised that all who come to Him in true faith and repentance will receive their sight, and, as we learn from John 9, it starts with the humility and the willingness to admit you need Jesus to open your eyes.

Spiritual Blindness Among Christians

Finally, it is crucial that we understand there is a kind of spiritual blindness that is cured at our conversion, but there is also a blindness that we are still susceptible to even as Christians. In his excellent book on leadership, Paul Tripp speaks of those in church leadership, but the principle applies to all Christians:

> If sin blinds, and it does, and if sin still remains in us, and
> it does, then, even as ministry leaders, there are pockets of

spiritual blindness in us. So, it is vital that we all forsake the thought that no one knows us better than we know ourselves. If there are places where we still suffer from spiritual blindness, then there are inaccuracies in the way we see ourselves and interpret our words and behavior. If, as a leader, you deny the possibility of personal spiritual blindness and trust the accuracy of your self-view, you are not humbly open and approachable to fellow leaders whom God has placed near you to help you see what you won't see on your own.[2]

Do not think that because Jesus has opened your eyes, and God has spoken light into your heart, that you can no longer fall into spiritual blindness. Sin is still deceitful. Satan is still prowling around like a lion. We must stay vigilant. Spiritual sight is a pursuit that never ends. Indeed, that is what this entire book is all about.

Remember the verses in Hebrews 3:12-13: 'Take care, brothers, lest there be in any of you an evil, unbelieving heart, leading you to fall away from the living God. But exhort one another every day, as long as it is called 'today,' that none of you may be hardened by the deceitfulness of sin.' Notice how the author of Hebrews connects the deceitfulness of sin to the warning of falling away from God. This is a warning for believers!

So, he says, we must take care. We must spend regular, consistent time with God in prayer and Bible reading. We must fellowship with other believers so that we can exhort one another and help one another hold on to Jesus. We must strive for 'the holiness without which no one will *see* the Lord' (Heb. 12:14). We must fight for spiritual sight because if we don't, we might lose it.

Pride

The sin which undergirds all this is pride. We could say this is the ultimate cause of spiritual blindness. From the Christian who sees no need for personal accountability, to the Pharisee who refuses to admit his need for Jesus to open his eyes, to the man unwilling to give up his sin, the common denominator among them all is their pride. In *Mere Christianity*, C. S. Lewis titled his chapter on pride, 'The Great Sin.' He writes, 'The essential vice, the utmost evil, is

---

2. Paul David Tripp, *Lead: 12 Gospel Principles for Leadership in the Church* (Wheaton: Crossway, 2020), 67.

pride. Unchastity, anger, greed, drunkenness, and all that, are mere flea-bites in comparison: it was through Pride that the devil became the devil: Pride leads to every other vice: it is the complete anti-God state of mind.'[3] Later, in the same chapter, he writes,

> In God you come up against something which is in every respect immeasurably superior to yourself. Unless you know God as that—and therefore, know yourself as nothing in comparison—you do not know God at all. As long as you are proud you cannot know God. A proud man is always looking down on things and people: and, of course, as long as you are looking down, you cannot see something that is above you.[4]

Therefore, humility is essential in our pursuit of seeing God. Jesus said 'Blessed are the poor in spirit, for theirs is the kingdom of heaven' (Matt. 5:3). In other words, the blessed person is the one who is spiritually needy and comes to the Lord with that posture in his heart. It is the tax collector, standing at a distance, beating his chest, crying out, 'God, have mercy on me, a sinner!' that went home justified, not the Pharisee who thanked God he was not like other sinful men. If you want to see God you must develop an understanding of your sinfulness and your need for God's mercy. Like the man born blind in John 9, you must acknowledge your blindness and cry out to Jesus to give you sight.

---

3. C. S. Lewis, *Mere Christianity, The Complete C. S. Lewis Signature Classics* (New York: HarperOne, 2002), 107-108.

4. Ibid., 105.

CHAPTER 10

SEEING GOD WHEN IT SEEMS HE IS NOT THERE

In his book, *The Creaking on the Stairs*, Mez McConnell shares the gut-wrenching account of the constant physical and emotional abuse he suffered as a child. It's a tough book to read, but I would heartily recommend it to all believers. One of the saddest parts of his story is what the constant abuse did to his view of God. He writes:

> I gave up on God when I was very young. It's not like I didn't believe He existed, I just didn't care anymore. He didn't seem relevant to me or my life. In fact, He didn't appear to have made one bit of difference to it. He never stopped the pain or abuse I went through, so what good was He? That was my reasoning and maybe it's yours. If God exists, then why let children suffer needlessly? Why let me be tortured day after day, year after year, throughout most of my childhood? So, either God didn't care about me and my pain or God couldn't do anything about me and my pain or God didn't exist.[1]

---

1.   Mez McConnell, *The Creaking On the Stairs: Finding Faith in God Through Childhood Abuse* (Ross-shire: Christian Focus, 2019), 42.

While many of us will never experience the trauma of Mez McConnell's childhood, it is universal that every Christian will go through seasons when it becomes difficult to see God at all. Perhaps it will be a period of unexplainable depression, the prolonged pain of grief after the tragic loss of a family member, months of stress at work, lack of sleep while caring for an infant, or simply one of those when-it-rains-it-pours seasons. However it comes, you can be sure it will. How can we fight to see God during the times when it honestly seems like He is not there? How can we prepare ourselves before those times arrive?

God Understands

Paul tells us that, 'All Scripture is God-breathed' (2 Tim. 3:16). As Christians, one of our foundational convictions about the Bible is that every word of it is from God. Even though the books of the Old and New Testaments come from around forty different authors, and were written over the course of approximately 1500 years, every word was inspired by God. It is one book, by one Author. Entire volumes have been written on the implications of this, but there is one which is especially important for us here, and hardly anything could be more encouraging when you are in the midst of a season when it seems God is not there. I think the most appropriate way to introduce this truth is through the Psalms.

The book of Psalms is like a prayer journal, and most of the psalms were written by David. What I have found so refreshing is David's blunt honesty as he cries out to God. 'Why, O Lord, do you stand far away? Why do you hide yourself in times of trouble?' (Ps. 10:1). 'How long, O Lord? Will you forget me forever? How long will you hide your face from me? How long must I take counsel in my soul and have sorrow in my heart all the day? How long shall my enemy be exalted over me?' (Ps. 13:1-2). See how David takes his frustrations and complaints directly to God? He's laying open his heart before the Lord. You might say David gives Him the God's honest truth. David is going through a season when it seems God is absent, and what does he do? He tells God about it.

But what makes this so encouraging to those of us struggling to see God is that God Himself inspired David to write these words! Remember, every word of Scripture is God-breathed. So, these are not just David's words, they are the very words of God. God *wanted*

David to write his complaints and frustrations. God *wanted* them to be preserved as inspired Scripture. Why? So that we could read them today and know that God understands. He knows there will be times when we feel like this. God is giving us permission to bring our honest frustrations and complaints directly to Him. He is graciously providing us with biblically-sanctioned words to express what we are feeling. He is preparing us for those seasons when it seems like He is not there.

The Bible is not a book full of sentimental and shallow answers to life's problems. Instead of dismissive ignorance, we find a gritty realism that looks evil directly in the face and does not turn away. Throughout the pages of God's Word, we often find the suffering of believers to be greater than that of unbelievers. God's people suffered such starvation and panic in the book of Lamentations that it led some women to eat their own children. Job experienced immeasurable loss and then had intense and prolonged physical suffering added to his emotional grief, all for being one of the most righteous men on earth. Jews and Christians were unjustly persecuted and punished for their faith in God time and time again. Anyone who claims the Bible does not provide a realistic look at life's problems simply has not read much of it. The fact that every word is from the mouth of God Himself is an immense encouragement. This is a God who understands.

So, do not be surprised when you experience a season when it seems God is not there. Expect them to come. You will go through periods of spiritual dryness, unanswered prayer, and extended times of having to wait on the Lord. He will *seem* distant and even absent at times. In reality, He is neither distant nor absent. As David wrote in Psalm 56, 'You have kept count of my tossings; put my tears in your bottle. Are they not in your book?' (Ps. 56:8). He sees and knows every detail of our struggles, but David's words in some other psalms show us that there will be times when it feels as if He is not paying attention. Prepare yourself now before those times come.

A Misplaced Idea of God's Presence

Perhaps a part of our struggle to see God could be the result of an unbiblical view of God's presence. When we feel as if God is not with us, we need to ask ourselves why we believe He is present at certain times and not present at others. I do not mean to imply it is sinful to experience what David experienced when he wrote Psalm 10 or Psalm 13. God compassionately gave those psalms to us because He knew there would be times when we feel like that. But have you ever stopped to analyze and critique why you believe God is present or not?

For example, when everything seems to be going great, some conclude it must mean God is looking down on them with favor. But you won't find warrant for that anywhere in the Bible. It might be true, but it might not. At times, Satan works to lull us into a false sense of confidence and then attacks when our guard is down. The path of the cross is rarely the easy, comfortable road. When a life decision initially leads to happiness, does that automatically mean it was the Lord's will? Not necessarily. Yet Christians are so quick to declare God's hand in the situation when things line up exactly as they wanted. Most of us, if we looked back on our lives, would find a number of instances when time revealed a certain decision or circumstance was not as pleasant as we initially thought. We ought to be slow and cautious in making confident assertions that surely a thing must have been from the Lord. Satan is skilled at reeling in gullible believers, or those whose emotions can be easily swayed.

Suffering

While comfort and ease do not necessarily imply the Lord's favor, we must also understand that suffering does not imply God's absence. On the contrary, there are many times in Scripture when suffering is the evidence of God's *presence*. Take Paul's thorn in the flesh. He pleaded with the Lord three times to have it removed, but God refused and said, 'My grace is sufficient for you, for my power is made perfect in weakness' (2 Cor. 12:9). Paul's suffering was an opportunity for God to show His strength through human weakness. God was right there the whole time, granting Paul the strength to endure.

In fact, Paul's life is one of the most poignant examples of this principle in all of Scripture. When the Lord spoke to Ananias and told him to go lay hands on Paul and grant him sight, He said, 'Go, for he is a chosen instrument of mine to carry my name before the Gentiles and kings and the children of Israel. For *I will show him how much he must suffer for the sake of my name*' (Acts 9:15-16, emphasis added). Paul's suffering was part of the deliberate plan of God, to glorify Himself among many.

Proverbs 17:3 says, 'The crucible is for silver, and the furnace is for gold, and the Lord tests hearts.' In other words, the way you purify or shape metals like silver or gold is with a super-hot furnace and a crucible to hold and pour them. Just as those things purify and change the shape of metals, the Lord purifies and changes the shape of hearts. And He does so through trials. Even our Lord had to experience suffering to reach perfection: 'For it was fitting that he, for whom and by whom all things exist, in bringing many sons to glory, should make the founder of their salvation perfect through suffering' (Heb. 2:10). Suffering is God's means of strengthening, purifying, and shaping us. Do not be surprised when it comes. And when it does, may it remind you that God is there, and He is working on you.

Suffering is not just an evidence of God's presence, but also a *pathway* to seeing God more clearly. As Paul recounts his sufferings in 2 Corinthians 11, we begin to realize one of the reasons this man had such an intimate knowledge of God is because of his great suffering. It is true of Job as well. He even understood it in the midst of his suffering: 'For I know that my Redeemer lives, and at the last he will stand upon the earth. And after my skin has been thus destroyed, yet in my flesh *I shall see God, whom I shall see for myself, and my eyes shall behold, and not another.* My heart faints within me' (Job 19:25-27, emphasis added)! Job's hope in the midst of great suffering was that he knew there was light at the end of the tunnel—the light, or *sight*, of God. The end of the book of Job shows us how Job's sufferings brought him to a knowledge and a sight of God that he could not have reached by any other means. Suffering was a pathway to seeing God more clearly.

We often find this to be the case with those who have suffered greatly, and have come out the other side. When I speak to men and women whom the Lord has carried through an intense trial, they exude an intimate knowledge and friendship with God that I long for myself. But how much do I really long for it? Enough to go through that level of suffering? I must admit, sometimes I am weak and afraid when I think of it.

Paul set a wonderful example for us in this area when he wrote, 'I want to know Christ and the power of his resurrection, and the fellowship of sharing in his sufferings' (Phil. 3:10). He longed to suffer as Christ suffered. Perhaps that is why the Apostles were rejoicing after being beaten for teaching about Jesus: 'and when they had called in the apostles, they beat them and charged them not to speak in the name of Jesus, and let them go. Then they left the presence of the council, rejoicing that they were counted worthy to suffer dishonor for the name' (Acts 5:40-41 They too, wanted to share in the sufferings of Christ, and when they did it gave them joy. Why? Because Jesus told them this would happen if they remained faithful. It was confirmation that they were being true to their Lord and friend! Their suffering was not evidence of God's absence, but of His presence! The world has no power over people who think like this.

The Psalm of Darkness

David is gritty and brutally honest as he writes in the psalms. We frequently see his despair, but almost every time, he includes a glimmer of hope. Enemies surround him, it seems like God is absent, but he holds on to his faith and trust in God's goodness. He will not give in completely.

However, there is one psalm that is darkness all the way through. No glimmer of hope. No light at the end of the tunnel. Of Psalm 88, Old Testament scholar Derek Kidner writes, 'There is no sadder prayer in the Psalter... there is hardly a spark of hope in the psalm itself.'[2] Yet this is one of my favorite psalms, and if you stare at it long enough, it yields one of the deepest comforts for sufferers and strugglers found in the entire Bible.

I would encourage you to take a few moments, open a Bible, and read through this psalm in its entirety. A full exposition of this psalm is beyond the scope of this chapter, but I believe you will get a sense of the comfort I mentioned above when you see just a few phrases.

> *You* have put me in the depths of the pit, in the regions dark and deep. *Your* wrath lies heavy upon me, and *you* overwhelm me with all *your* waves. [Selah] *You* have caused my companions to shun me; *you* have made me a horror to them. I am shut in so that I cannot escape.' (Ps. 88:6-8 emphasis added)

2. Derek Kidner, *Psalms 73-150: An Introduction and Commentary*, vol. 16, Tyndale Old Testament Commentaries (Downers Grove: InterVarsity, 1975), 348.

Do you see how all of this comes directly from the Lord? This is where we find the great comfort. *Comfort?! What comfort?! This sounds soul-crushing!* Understandable. But our knowledge of God's character helps us immensely here. We know that God is good, benevolent, gentle, and loving. Everything He sends our way is for our good (Rom. 8:28). He cares for us and does not leave us to the storms of this world.

Not only that, but we know that He works through trials and suffering to purify and shape us. This is why Paul writes, 'We rejoice in our sufferings, knowing that suffering produces endurance, and endurance produces character, and character produces hope' (Rom. 5:3-4).

And James writes, 'Count it all joy, my brothers, when you meet trials of various kinds, for you know that the testing of your faith produces steadfastness. And let steadfastness have its full effect, that you may be perfect and complete, lacking in nothing' (Jas 1:2-4).

If our tests, trials, and sufferings come from God, they can be nothing but His loving pruning or purifying. Therefore, even when it seems the darkness will not lift, we can know God is still being good to us. It doesn't feel like it, but it is true. 'God is treating you as sons... he disciplines us for our good, that we may share in his holiness. For the moment all discipline seems painful rather than pleasant, but later it yields the peaceful fruit of righteousness to those who have been trained by it' (Heb. 12:7, 10-11).

And remember, the words of Psalm 88 are not just the words of David; they are the very words of God Himself. That means God wanted them in the Bible. He wanted them there for you to read. Why would God put a psalm in His Word that has no glimmer of hope? No light at the end of the tunnel? Because He knew you would experience times like that, times where it seems the darkness will never lift. Psalm 88 is telling us the Lord is there, in the darkest despair, shaping us into more effective vessels for His glory.

Spiritual Dry Spells

If you walk with Christ for years you will experience periods of spiritual dryness. The Scriptures do not make your heart sing as they once did. Corporate worship does not invigorate your soul like it used to. In times like these our fire for God seems as if it is smoldering at best, and it can be especially hard to see Him.

But there is an encouragement here that we should not miss. When a Christian man or woman has walked with God for some time, and begins to mature in their faith, God will often allow them to experience certain trials from which He has shielded them during the infancy of their faith. This makes perfect sense when we think of it. For a new believer, it is important that they experience frequent answers to prayer and encouragements not to fall away. There is a sense of newness in their Bible study, and their growth curve is steep. But as the years pass, God wants their trust in Him to become less and less dependent on their feelings. He does not want saplings with shallow roots, easily blown by the wind. He wants oaks of righteousness able to endure the storms and droughts. Craig Troxel, author and professor at Westminster Seminary, writes,

> Every Christian undergoes an extended low time when all the sweetness of Christ's presence seems distant and his support seems absent. Such seasons assess our heart to see if we will, as C. S. Lewis expresses it, 'carry out from the will alone duties which have lost all relish.' Will we obey even though we do not feel like it? God is teaching us how to walk, and so, from time to time, he withdraws his hand to see what we can do. In times like that, we become unusually useful to the king (and dangerous to the enemy)—because we are obeying whether we feel incentives or not, we are praying even though the petitions feel dry, and we are seeking the good of others when it is of no advantage to us. This is true commitment. It is a mark of sterling obedience from the heart's will.[3]

The experience of spiritual dryness is often another sign of God's fatherly testing and, therefore, it can be an encouraging sign of His presence. Now, do not be deceived: If you neglect spiritual disciplines like prayer, Bible reading, corporate worship, and fellowship with other believers, your spiritual dryness will no doubt be a by-product of your own actions. But there will be times where dryness will come even as we are abiding in the Lord. Puritan author John Owen writes, 'While we are in this life, the Lord Christ is pleased, in His sovereign wisdom, sometimes to withdraw, and, as it were,

---

3. A. Craig Troxel, *With All Your Heart: Orienting Your Mind, Desires, and Will Toward Christ* (Wheaton: Crossway, 2020), 140.

to hide Himself from us.'[4] As Isaiah says, 'Truly, you are a God who hides himself' (Is. 45:15). In those seasons, press on with the encouragement that God very well may be deepening your roots, and anchoring your faith in something stronger than your feelings.

Feelings

Speaking of feelings, God's presence and our feelings of His presence have very little correlation. Christians today desperately need to learn this. Not only was that mountaintop experience a 'God thing,' but so was the period of spiritual dryness you went through a few months ago, or the four days you spent in bed due to sickness, or the inner battle with bitterness that has lasted for years. Do not equate God's presence with your feelings of His presence. In fact, we often have to correct our feelings with the truth of what Martin Luther called the *external Word*.

Martyn Lloyd-Jones, in his classic *Spiritual Depression*, challenged believers to refuse to passively listen to their feelings and the thoughts that naturally come into their minds. He wrote, 'Have you realized that most of your unhappiness in life is due to the fact that you are listening to yourself instead of talking to yourself?'[5] He goes on to explain what he means by referring back to David's words in Psalm 42 and 43:

> Now this man's treatment was this; instead of allowing this self to talk to him, he starts talking to himself. 'Why art thou cast down, O my soul?' he asks. His soul had been depressing him, crushing him. So, he stands up and says: 'Self, listen for a moment, I will speak to you'... you have to address yourself, preach to yourself, question yourself.[6]

Instead of allowing our feelings to dictate to us and determine our ability to see God, we take hold of God's external Word and preach it to ourselves. We correct our feelings. As Paul says, 'We demolish arguments and every pretension that sets itself up against the knowledge of God, and we take captive every thought to make it obedient to Christ. (2 Cor. 10:5, NIV84).

---

4. John Owen, *The Glory of Christ* (East Peoria: Banner of Truth, 2018), 109.

5. D. Martyn Lloyd-Jones, *Spiritual Depression: Its Causes and Cure* (Grand Rapids: Eerdmans, 1965), 20.

6. Ibid., 21.

The Hidden Hand of God

One of the unique and distinguishing marks of the book of Esther is that God is not explicitly mentioned anywhere in the book. Not even once. At first glance, it seems strange that such a book would be included in the canon of the Old Testament, but anyone who reads it immediately understands why. The story of Esther, Mordecai, and the Jews is a masterclass in God's providential work behind the scenes to bring about His purposes and His glory. It seems like God is not there, yet when we look closer, with biblically trained eyes, we can see Him clearly and gloriously. Esther is a microcosm for what I am attempting to show you in this chapter.

There is only one scene in all of Scripture that makes this point more powerfully than the book of Esther: the death of Jesus on the cross. Remember Mez McConnell, from the beginning of the chapter? Well, in his wonderful book, he recounts the story of his implausible conversion to Jesus Christ. Against all odds, and in spite of Satan's intense effort, that abused and tormented boy grew up to become a minister of the gospel. He wrote this:

> The crucifixion of Jesus looked like the biggest miscarriage of justice in history. It looked like God was asleep at the wheel. It looked like He didn't care. When in fact, His was the hidden hand behind it all. Now, I appreciate that many people don't like this. They can't bring themselves to accept that God permits evil to happen. But God is sovereign over all things. Even over our abuse. Especially over our abuse.[7]

The cross is the most poignant and vivid example in human history of a time where it seemed like God was not there. 'My God, my God, why have you forsaken me?' (Matt. 27:46). Yet this was *the moment* of God's glorious presence and activity. When it seems like God is not there, remember, Jesus experienced that feeling as well, to a much greater degree. And for Him, God's presence was not only in His hidden providence, but in His active crushing of His Son (Is. 53:10). Jesus was not mistaken for His feeling that God had forsaken Him. It was true. God poured out the full force of His wrath against sin on His Son. He was forsaken so that we would never be forsaken. He took God's wrath so that we would never have to fear it coming to us.

---

7. McConnell, *Creaking*, 182.

As the bystanders mocked Jesus, and told Him to call on His God to save Him, what they did not see was that saving Him wasn't the plan. Crushing Him was. God was powerfully present the whole time, just not in the way everyone expected.

CHAPTER 11

THE PURE IN HEART

What does it take to see God? We have seen the negative side of the coin as we examined the things that keep us from seeing God in chapter eight. But until now we have not given an extended and concentrated look at the positive side. What will help us to see God? Or, to put it another way, to what kind of person does God delight to show Himself? Jesus answers for us at the beginning of the Sermon on the Mount: 'Blessed are the pure in heart, for they shall see God' (Matt. 5:8).

Now, first we must acknowledge that in the Bible there were a number of instances where God showed Himself to someone who was not looking for Him, and had no particular desire to see Him. We might think of Abraham, Jacob, Joseph, Solomon, or Ezekiel in the Old Testament. In the New Testament, the dramatic conversion of Paul on the road to Damascus is a prime example. But again, in this book we are not pursuing a physical sight of God but a spiritual one. For that, we turn to Jesus' words at the beginning of the Sermon on the Mount, commonly referred to as *The Beatitudes*: 'Blessed are the pure in heart, for they shall see God' (Matt. 5:8).

What does it mean to be pure in heart? Is it possible to attain in this life? Is the promise of seeing God only for eternity, or is it also for our lives now? These are the questions to which we now turn.

Moral Purity

The first thing that likely comes to our minds when we think of this purity of heart is moral purity, and this is indeed a large part of what Jesus meant. It is similar to the words of the Lord's brother James when he wrote that true religion that pleases God (along with caring for orphans and widows) is to 'keep oneself *unstained* from the world' (Jas. 1:27, emphasis added). Some translations use the word *undefiled*. God has called us to be holy as He is holy. Holy simply means to be set apart from the world and its sinfulness.

So, when Jesus says only the pure in heart will see God, He is telling us that we cannot keep a foot in the sin of the world and expect to experience the blessing of God's glory at the same time. Paul said, 'You cannot drink the cup of the Lord and the cup of demons. You cannot partake of the table of the Lord and the table of demons' (1 Cor. 10:21). You cannot have it both ways. You cannot live a worldly life characterized by sin and expect to see God. The Apostle John wrote, 'No one who keeps on sinning has either seen him or known him' (1 John 3:6), and later, 'Whoever does evil has not seen God' (3 John 11).

Now, notice the implication in those last two verses from John's letters. No one who keeps on sinning has seen God. The one who does evil has not seen God. This implies there are those who have seen Him! Remember, this is the same Apostle John that twice wrote, 'No one has ever seen God' (John 1:18, 1 John 4:12). Is he contradicting himself? Not if there are two kinds of sight. No one has ever seen God with their physical eyes, but those who keep themselves from the evil of this world and thus purify their hearts have set themselves on a path to see Him. Of course, this does not mean God requires perfection. We will never reach perfect purity until we see Him face to face. But what He does require is the pursuit of purity from the heart.

To see God, we must be pursuing holiness. Do not listen to anyone who tells you the Lord is not concerned with holy obedience. This is a natural and common-occurring distortion of the truth of God's grace, but it is a dangerous one. As the Apostle Paul teaches in the book of Romans, grace does not lead to a disregard of God's commands, but a greater obedience! Without moral purity, we will not see the Lord. Psalm 11:7 says, 'For the Lord is righteous; he loves righteous deeds; *the upright shall behold his face*' (Ps. 11:7, emphasis added). And the author of Hebrews writes, 'Strive for peace with everyone, and *for the holiness without which no one will see the Lord*' (Heb. 12:14, emphasis added).

Our Inner Being

Note what Jesus did not say in Matthew 5:8. He did not say those who are pure in their actions would see God. It is rather those who are pure in their hearts. If you follow the Sermon on the Mount over the course of Matthew chapters 5-7, you will find this is a recurrent theme. Jesus is calling us to a much deeper obedience than simply obeying the letter of the law with our outward actions. He wants our hearts. This is why He would go on to say, 'For I tell you, unless your righteousness exceeds that of the scribes and Pharisees, you will never enter the kingdom of heaven' (Matt. 5:20). The scribes and Pharisees were models of outward obedience, but on the inside they were rotten (see Matthew 23:25-28).

In Psalm 51 David writes, 'Behold, you delight in truth in the inward being, and you teach me wisdom in the secret heart' (Ps. 51:6). This is David's psalm of confession, written after his adultery with Bathsheba and subsequent murder of her husband were exposed. He had kept it a secret for many months until God drew it out of him through the prophet Nathan. But keeping sin a secret is never successful. 'Be sure, your sin will find you out' (Num. 32:23). David's sin found him out, and it taught him a painful but important lesson: sin is much more about our inner being than our actions. David's sin began in the heart. He saw Bathsheba on the rooftop and lusted after her. Therefore, he understood, God is not satisfied with merely purity of actions. He delights in purity 'in the secret heart.'

Every sin has its root in the heart. Take pornography as an example. A man who is addicted to looking at pornography must take immediate and drastic measures to prevent himself from accessing it. He must manipulate his outward behavior. But if his efforts remain at the level of his actions, he will never experience victory over it. The only way to truly put it to death and find freedom is to go to the heart. Why does he desire it in his heart? Why does his heart prefer the temporary, sinful pleasures of pornography over the lasting and more satisfying pleasures of God? Sin begins in the heart, and it will only be defeated at the heart-level.

Jesus taught this a number of times. For example, Jesus said, 'But what comes out of the mouth proceeds from the heart, and this defiles a person. For out of the heart come evil thoughts, murder, adultery, sexual immorality, theft, false witness, slander' (Matt. 15:18-19). Martyn Lloyd-Jones once said that people in this world think their main problem is outside of themselves and the solution is within. But the Bible tells us our main problem is within ourselves, and the solution is outside of us, namely Christ.

Undivided and Undiluted

When Jesus spoke of the heart that is pure, He not only meant one that is morally unstained from worldliness, but one that is undivided and undiluted. The idea is that we would have a single-minded devotion to God. The pure heart is one without hypocrisy, or as Danish philosopher and theologian Søren Kierkegaard[1] put it, 'purity of heart is to will one thing.' In Psalm 24, David writes, 'Who shall ascend the hill of the Lord? And who shall stand in his holy place? He who has clean hands and a pure heart, who does not lift up his soul to what is false and does not swear deceitfully' (Ps. 24:3-4). David could have begun that Psalm by saying, *'Who shall see the Lord?'*

Consider something like olive oil. Often on the bottle you will see the claim that this is '100% pure olive oil.' In other words, it has not been diluted or mixed with any other kind of oil or liquid. What's inside the bottle is just one thing, not two. It is pure and undivided. Such are the hearts of those who will see God. Craig Troxel, in his book *With All Your Heart*, writes,

> The pure heart is intent on serving the Lord alone, while the divided heart seeks to serve the Lord plus something else. Joshua exhorted Israel to 'choose this day' to serve either the true and living God or the gods 'beyond the River' or in Canaan (Josh. 24:14-15). Elijah told Israel to stop 'limping between two different opinions' and either follow the Lord or follow Baal (1 Kings 18:21). Jesus exposed the fallacy of having two conflicting loyalties: 'No one can serve two masters, for either he will hate the one and love the other,

---

1. Søren Kierkegaard, *Purity of Heart is to Will One Thing: Spiritual Preparation for the Office of Confession* (San Francisco: HarperOne, 1956).

or he will be devoted to the one and despise the other. You
cannot serve God and money' (Matthew 6:24).[2]

In Psalm 86, David asks God for such a heart: 'Teach me your way,
O Lord, and I will walk in your truth; give me an undivided heart,
that I may fear your name' (Ps. 86:11, NIV84). David is asking
God to grant him a heart that is undivided—single-minded and
completely devoted in its pursuit of Him. In the ESV it says 'unite
my heart.' In other words, take the duplicity and disarray of my
heart and center it on a solitary pursuit. No hypocrisy.

The Fear of the Lord

An essential part of what it means to have a pure heart, as Jesus
spoke of in Matthew 5:8, is the fear of the Lord. Now, initially you
might think that purity of heart and the fear of the Lord are not
inherently connected, but I am going to argue here that they are.
You cannot be pure in heart without having a proper fear of the
Lord. Therefore, without the fear of the Lord you cannot see God.
Let me show you the connection.

You have already seen one link in the chain: Psalm 86:11. David
prays, 'Give me an undivided heart, that I may fear your name.' The
pure heart is undivided in its devotion to the Lord, and David's
prayer shows us that the purpose of a pure, or undivided, heart is a
proper fear of the Lord. This makes perfect sense when we consider
that 'the fear of the Lord is the beginning of wisdom' (Prov. 9:10).
In fact, Jesus' words in Matthew 5:8 imply that the end of wisdom
is seeing God.

What is the fear of the Lord? Perhaps the best study on this
subject is the excellent *Rejoice and Tremble* by Michael Reeves.
Reeves shows from Scripture that the fear of the Lord is not what
our common use of the word *fear* today would imply. It is not a
constant anxiety or worrisome dread, but rather a healthy and even
happy enjoyment of God as our creator and redeemer. It is an awe-
filled worship and loving devotion mixed with a serious appreciation
for what God can and will do to His enemies.

The second link in the chain connecting the fear of the Lord
to Jesus' statement on the pure in heart is Psalm 19:9, which says
'the fear of the Lord is pure, enduring forever' (NIV84). The ESV

2.　Troxel, *With All Your Heart*, 98.

translation says it is 'clean,' which implies the same idea. Fearing the Lord is a condition of the heart, and since the fear of the Lord is itself pure, clean, and undiluted, it requires a heart that is pure as well. So, it follows then, only one with a pure heart can properly fear the Lord. But it is also true that without the fear of the Lord our hearts will not be pure or undivided. Purity of heart and the fear of the Lord are so inherently connected, you cannot have one without the other. Therefore, without the fear of the Lord, you cannot see God.

Consider God's Word through the prophet Isaiah: 'This is the one to whom I will look: he who is humble and contrite in spirit and trembles at my word' (Is. 66:2). As you study the fear of the Lord in Scripture you will find that it includes humility and contrition. It includes a deep, joyful but serious reverence for God's Word— a trembling. God says this is the kind of person to whom He will look. This is the kind of person God will favor or bless. This is the kind of person to whom God will reveal Himself. They will see God.

This person is humble. They have a proper view of themselves because their eyes are constantly on the magnificence, the power, the glory, and the grace of God. They have remorse for their sins. Their loving fear of God produces grief in their heart when they do anything to offend Him. And they tremble at His Word. They revere it. They honor it. They hold it in high esteem. They read and study and seek to know it with all their hearts, and then they seek to obediently apply it to their lives.

Both Now and in Eternity

When I read Jesus' words in Matthew 5:8, that the pure in heart will see God, I immediately think of eternity. We will see God face to face in the new heaven and the new earth. This is true; gloriously true, in fact! But it is not all. As I combed through the commentaries on this verse, nearly every one of them noted how there is an aspect of seeing God now in what Jesus said.

For example, John Stott writes: 'Only the pure in heart will see God, see him now with the eye of faith and see his glory in the hereafter, for only the utterly sincere can bear the dazzling vision in whose light the darkness of deceit must vanish and by whose fire all shams are burned up.'[3] Matthew Henry writes, 'It is the perfection of the soul's happiness to *see God; seeing him,* as we may by faith in our present state, is a *heaven upon earth.*[4] Seeing God with the eyes of our hearts is a precursor and foreshadowing of the unfiltered sight of His glory we will experience in eternity.

As we examine the Beatitudes in Matthew 5:3-12, we find that each one of Jesus' promises contains a note of partial fulfillment in this life, and complete fulfillment in eternity. The kingdom of God belongs to the poor in spirit; those who mourn will be comforted; those who hunger and thirst for righteousness will be satisfied; the peacemakers will be called sons of God. Do you see? For those who are following Christ with sincere faith, these things are true of us now, even as they will be more fully realized after our death and resurrection.

Only with Jesus

There still remains one question we have not addressed: is purity of heart actually possible in this life? Perhaps, like me, your initial answer is, *'I'm not sure if it's possible for others, but I certainly do not feel like my heart is pure!'* When David says in Psalm 17:3, 'You have tried my heart, you have visited me by night, you have tested me, and you will find nothing,' I honestly feel like I cannot relate. I could not say that with a clear conscience before God!

To make matters worse, there are a number of places in Scripture which imply no one has a pure heart before the Lord. For example, 'The heart is deceitful above all things, and desperately sick; who can understand it?' (Jer. 17:9). Or, 'Who can say, "I have made my heart pure; I am clean from my sin?"' (Prov. 20:9). The clear, implied answer to this rhetorical question from Proverbs is 'No one.' Is purity of heart actually possible before we are transformed and perfected for eternity? If not, is everything I have said about seeing God undone?

It is crucial to understand, when it comes to these two verses above, that they speak of the heart of all unbelievers—the unregenerate heart. It is the heart of someone without Christ. But when we are

---

3. John R. W. Stott, *The Message of the Sermon on the Mount,* The Bible Speaks Today (Downers Grove: InterVarsity, 1985), 49.

4. Matthew Henry, *Matthew Henry's Commentary on the Whole Bible: Complete and Unabridged in One Volume* (Peabody: Hendrickson, 1994), 1630. Emphasis on the original.

born again in Christ, God gives us a new heart. Speaking of the new covenant that God was going to make wiht His people, God speaks through Ezekiel and says, 'And I will give you a new heart, and a new spirit I will put within you. And I will remove the heart of stone from your flesh and give you a heart of flesh' (Eze. 36:26). A heart of flesh, that feels what it is supposed to feel, rather than an unfeeling heart of stone. Only with new hearts can we attain to the purity of heart that Jesus spoke of in Matthew 5:8.

In some ways, after our new birth, our hearts are radically changed and the difference is immediate and significant. In other ways, the change is gradual as our hearts begin to learn the ways of God. God *gradually* helps us to feel what He feels in our hearts— to love what He loves, and to hate what He hates. But the purity that Jesus speaks of can be true of any believer, no matter how immature or new in the faith. Imagine someone who is converted to Christ out of a life characterized by sexual promiscuity, alcohol abuse, compulsive lying, theft, and selfish pride. Suppose their repentance is genuine and their conversion is real at the heart-level. Then suppose, a week after their baptism, they die in a car accident. Was their heart completely free of sinful desire? Probably not. Will they see God in eternal life? Absolutely. The purity of heart Jesus speaks of is not only possible in this life, it is possible from the first moment of our new birth.

We see elsewhere in the New Testament that this is so. For example, Acts 15:9 tells us that those who have been reborn in Christ have had 'their hearts cleansed by faith.' Paul says, 'But thanks be to God, that you who were once slaves of sin have become *obedient from the heart* to the standard of teaching to which you were committed' (Rom. 6:17, emphasis added). And places like 1 Timothy 1:5, 2 Timothy 2:22, and 1 Peter 1:22 all speak of believers acting 'from a pure heart.'

So yes, purity of heart is possible in this present life, here and now. And therefore, so is seeing God. Will we ever be completely pure, or morally perfect, in this life? Of course not. But we can and should be striving for and growing in holiness in such a way that it can honestly be said of us that we keep our hearts unstained, undivided, and pure in our pursuit of Jesus.

CHAPTER 12

THE LIGHT THAT GIVES SIGHT

In the first book of *The Lord of the Rings* trilogy, Frodo Baggins and his eight other companions embark on their quest to take the evil ring of Sauron into his own land, the land of Mordor, and destroy it in the only place it can be destroyed, the fires inside Mount Doom. After a treacherous journey through the mines of Moria, where they lose their mighty leader, the wizard Gandalf, the company finds refuge in the forest of Lothlorien, the home of the elves. The elves are strong and cunning warriors, and fellow enemies of the dark lord Sauron. The greatest of all the elves is Lady Galadriel. She warmly welcomes the company into her realm, but her supernatural gaze pierces their thoughts and the intents of their hearts. Through her understanding and foresight, she comes to discern what each companion most needs to complete his journey. Before they part ways, she presents them all with gifts fit for each of them. Frodo is given his gift last:

> 'And you, Ring-bearer,' she said, turning to Frodo. 'I come to you last who are not last in my thoughts. For you I have prepared this.' She held up a small crystal phial: it glittered as she moved it, and rays of white light sprang from her hand. 'In this phial,' she said, 'is caught the light of Eärendil's star, set amid the waters of my fountain. It will shine still brighter

when night is about you. May it be a light to you in dark places, when all other lights go out.[1]

A light in dark places when all other lights go out. This is a fitting description of the treasure God has given to every believer in His Word. Light is an important theme throughout the Bible, and it is consistently tied to spiritual sight. Those who walk in darkness cannot see where they are going, nor can they see the Lord (John 12:35; 1 John 2:11). But there is a spiritual light from God that allows His people to see Him, and to properly see the world around them. In this chapter we will take a brief look at the theme of light throughout the story of the Bible.

Let There Be Light

Of course, the proper place to start in a biblical study of light, is in the beginning. The first recorded words of God in the Bible are, 'Let there be light' (Gen. 1:3). We know these were more than mere spoken words. These words had a creative, explosive power unlike any force the universe has ever seen! It was a power to create something out of nothing. God is the only one of whom the saying is literally and unfailingly true: When He speaks, things happen.

Genesis 1:1-2 clearly shows us light was not the first creative act of God. The best and most logical interpretation of those first verses is that Genesis 1:1-2 describes God's first act of creation—the universe, including the earth—and then the verses that follow describe how He brought form and order to it. So, light was not the first thing God created. However, it is nevertheless the first time we are told something was created by the powerful force of God's spoken word. It would stand to reason that the formless and void earth and the heavens were also created by God's voice, but it is telling that God intentionally chose those words, 'Let there be light,' to be His first recorded words in all of Scripture.

Those words—let there be light—are not just a record of God's first words, they are a microcosm for the entire story of the Bible. The Bible is God's self-revelation to us. Without it we would not know who He is, nor could we rightly understand ourselves and the world we live in. So, the Bible is God saying, 'Let there be light' to the human race. We can be confident that God was intentional in

---

1. J. R. R. Tolkien, *The Lord of the Rings: One Volume* (Boston: Houghton Mifflin Harcourt, 2012), 376.

this because of the emphasis that He places on the theme of light throughout the rest of Scripture.

In Your Light Do We See Light

David understood that God not only said, 'Let there be light,' to the dark void, but He was saying it to all men and women through His Word. We see this in his words from Psalm 36, 'In your light do we see light' (Ps. 36:9). This short sentence is so deep and insightful, it warrants an extended look. What does David mean that in God's light we see light?

The first thing that will help us is understanding that *light* is another way of saying truth, or a knowledge of the truth. Therefore, David is telling us that only with a knowledge of God's truth do we come to any knowledge of any truth. Without God's truth, all of our so-called knowledge will be mistaken, distorted, skewed, or all of the above. At the judgment, the 'wisdom' of this world will be exposed for the folly it really is (see 1 Corinthians 1:18-31).

You cannot see and properly appreciate truth or beauty without the knowledge of God. You cannot understand yourself or the world rightly until you see by the light of God: His Word. Furthermore, no one can even see or think or understand anything at all without the body and brain and abilities that God gives and even sustains. The atheist can only think blasphemous thoughts by means of the brain God provided and continues to sustain. He can only utter blasphemous words by means of the mouth and tongue God provided and continues to sustain. As John Piper writes,

> All existence and all knowledge depend on God. If we have life, we live by him. 'In him we live and move and have our being' (Acts 17:28). If we have any knowledge, we know by him. 'From him and through him and to him are all things' (Romans 11:36). We do not shed light on him by the light we see. He is the origin, the source. If we have any measure of light, it is he who is shedding light on what we see, not we.[2]

It is also true that God's light is like the light of the sun. Without it, we walk in darkness and we do not see where we are going

---

2. John Piper, *A Peculiar Glory: How the Christian Scriptures Reveal Their Complete Truthfulness* (Wheaton: Crossway, 2016), 160.

(John 12:35; 1 John 2:11), but with it we can clearly see everything else. Its light is what gives us the ability to see everything around us properly. C. S. Lewis once wrote, 'I believe in Christianity as I believe that the Sun has risen not only because I see it but because by it I see everything else.'[3]

Light in the Books of John

The Apostle John uses the theme of light more than any other biblical author. This is not surprising because we learn in John's gospel account that he is 'the disciple whom Jesus loved' (John 13:23; 19:26; 20:2; 21:7; 20). Apparently, John was closer to Jesus than anyone else. It makes sense then, that as Jesus consistently referred to Himself as the light from God sent into the world, John would pick up on that theme and feature it prominently in his writings. As you read his New Testament books, it seems clear that this was one of his favorite illustrations to communicate the way that Jesus revealed the glory of God to the world. In the prologue to John's account of Jesus' life he writes,

> In him was life, and the life was the light of men. The light shines in the darkness, and the darkness has not overcome it. There was a man sent from God, whose name was John. He came as a witness, to bear witness about the light, that all might believe through him. He was not the light, but came to bear witness about the light. The true light, which gives light to everyone, was coming into the world. (John 1:4-9)

John immediately clarifies the theme of light in the Bible by showing us that Jesus is the ultimate embodiment of God's light given to mankind. As we saw in chapter four, Jesus was the physical, visible embodiment of the invisible God no one has ever seen. Having established Jesus as the true light that has come into the world, John goes on to record a number of Jesus' own statements where He refers to Himself as this light. For example, in a passage we have already examined in a previous chapter, Jesus says to Nicodemus,

> And this is the judgment: the light has come into the world, and people loved the darkness rather than the light because their works were evil. For everyone who does wicked things

---

3. C. S. Lewis, *Is Theology Poetry* (Samizdat University Press, 2014), 15. http://www.samizdat.qc.ca/arts/lit/Theology=Poetry_CSL.pdf, accessed April 30, 2021.

hates the light and does not come to the light, lest his works should be exposed. But whoever does what is true comes to the light, so that it may be clearly seen that his works have been carried out in God. (John 3:19-21)

Jesus' entrance into the world was God speaking, 'Let there be light,' into the darkness. But, as Jesus told Nicodemus, while some welcomed the light, most recoiled at it. I once heard someone say that light draws the lost and weary traveler but it causes cockroaches to scatter. So it is with God's light. It exposes us and reveals our sin. As we all know, our natural tendency is to try and hide our sin— to keep it in the dark. Yet, we do not realize we are only hurting ourselves as we do this. God's exposing light is uncomfortable at first, but like a surgery to remove cancer, it is a good pain that leads to healing. In Psalm 90:8, Moses prays about how our secret sins are revealed by the light of God's presence.

In John 8:12, Jesus says of Himself, 'I am the light of the world. Whoever follows me will not walk in darkness, but will have the light of life' (John 8:12; cf. John 9:5). And later, 'The light is among you for a little while longer. Walk while you have the light, lest darkness overtake you. The one who walks in the darkness does not know where he is going. While you have the light, believe in the light, that you may become sons of light' (John 12:35-36).

In that last passage, Jesus begins to speak about the importance of believing in this light. His light is similar to sunlight in that by it you can see everything else clearly, but there is a crucial difference between the light of the sun and Jesus' light. The sun's light is there for all to see, and everyone can see it without trying. Not so with the light of Christ. You must *believe in* this light. You must open your heart to it and invite it in. You must put your trust and your hope in Jesus to see this light. As He said in John 12, 'I have come into the world as light, so that whoever believes in me may not remain in darkness' (John 12:46). We can only see this light by faith.

In 1 John, the Apostle consistently urges those who would read his letter to walk in the light. For example, 'But if we walk in the light, as he is in the light, we have fellowship with one another, and the blood of Jesus his Son cleanses us from all sin' (1 John 1:7). To walk in the light means to trust in Christ and to live according to the knowledge of God that He revealed. It is the equivalent of abiding in Christ as Jesus commanded in places like John 15:5. There are many virtues that characterize those who walk in the light, but the definitive one is love.

> At the same time, it is a new commandment that I am writing to you, which is true in him and in you, because the darkness is passing away and the true light is already shining. Whoever says he is in the light and hates his brother is still in darkness. Whoever loves his brother abides in the light, and in him there is no cause for stumbling. (1 John 2:8-10)

Our Light

In chapters four through six we saw that there are three primary ways God allows Himself to be seen by those who have the eyes to see: the Bible, Jesus, and other human beings. It follows, then, that these three are also the primary means of God giving His light to the world. We have already seen how God gives light to mankind through the Bible and through His Son Jesus. But Scripture also speaks of Christians as light. For example, in the Sermon on the Mount, Jesus said,

> You are the *light* of the world. A city set on a hill cannot be hidden. Nor do people light a lamp and put it under a basket, but on a stand, and it gives *light* to all in the house. In the same way, let *your light* shine before others, so that they may see your good works and give glory to your Father who is in heaven. (Matt. 5:14-16, emphasis added)

We would expect Jesus to call Himself the light of the world, as He did in John 8. But here, He says that we are the light of the world as well! How astounding is this? Surely, I do not deserve to be referred to in the same terms as Jesus Himself. And yet, it is right there in the pages of Scripture. It is true! God's people are the light of the world.

Now, when we think about the gaping chasm between our holiness and that of Jesus, we may feel we do not deserve to wear this title. But when we consider how we are ambassadors for Christ, and how God has ordained that unbelievers learn of Him through the lives and witness of His followers, it makes perfect sense. Paul speaks of this in his letter to the Ephesians:

116

> For at one time you were darkness, but now you are light
> in the Lord. Walk as children of light (for the fruit of light
> is found in all that is good and right and true), and try
> to discern what is pleasing to the Lord. Take no part in
> the unfruitful works of darkness, but instead expose them.
> For it is shameful even to speak of the things that they
> do in secret. But when anything is exposed by the light, it
> becomes visible, for anything that becomes visible is light.
> (Eph. 5:8-14)

Through us, God is exposing the things hidden in darkness, and
not simply exposing them, but making them into more lights! Do
you see how he says in verse 14, 'for anything that becomes visible
is light?' In other words, when we come to the light of Christ by
faith, we *become* one of God's lights. As Paul says in Philippians,
we are 'children of God without blemish in the midst of a crooked
and twisted generation, *among whom you shine as lights in the world*'
(Phil. 2:15, emphasis added).

The Light that Gives Sight

We have seen that the Bible is essentially God saying, 'Let there
be light,' to the human race. But those ancient words are not just the
story of Scripture, they are the story of salvation. In 2 Corinthians 4,
Paul tells us that our new birth in Christ is the result of God saying,
'Let there be light,' into our hearts.

> In their case the god of this world has blinded the minds of
> the unbelievers, to keep them from seeing the light of the
> gospel of the glory of Christ, who is the image of God. For
> what we proclaim is not ourselves, but Jesus Christ as Lord,
> with ourselves as your servants for Jesus' sake. For God, who
> said, 'Let light shine out of darkness,' has shone in our hearts
> to give the light of the knowledge of the glory of God in the
> face of Jesus Christ. (2 Cor. 4:4-6)

Satan is doing all that he can to keep people from seeing the light
of the gospel. God has sent Jesus to give the world light and He has
provided us with His light in the Scriptures, but there is still the
matter of the heart. As Jesus said, people love the darkness rather
than the light. They are blinded by pride and love for sin. It is not
enough that the light is in the world. As we saw above, people must
believe in the light. They must come to faith in Jesus.

I am a full-time minister in a church. My main task is to proclaim this light, whether it is publicly on a Sunday morning, or privately in conversations with individuals or small groups. One thing becomes crystal clear when you step into the role of minister as your vocation: you cannot change anyone's heart. I ache and pray for people to have the eyes of their hearts enlightened (Eph. 1:18), to come to see the light of Jesus and be saved, but I can only do so much. They must take the final step. They must repent. They must put their faith and trust in Christ. They must decide to follow Him.

But only God can awaken someone's heart to their desperate need of Him. Only God can shake someone out of their spiritual apathy. Once that happens, and someone puts their faith in Jesus and repents of their sin, only God can cause them to be born again. This is why, even though I firmly believe that a person must make a decision to follow Jesus, I still pray for God to say, 'Let there be light,' in the hearts of those who are still walking in darkness. I pray for God to open their hearts like He did Lydia's in Acts 16:14. Yes, God has given His light to the world in the form of Jesus, and the Bible, and even other Christians. But those who are lost still need Him to give them the light that leads to sight. Only God can say, 'Let there be light,' into the darkness of the human heart.

When All Other Lights Go Out

As our study of light in the Bible appropriately began in the beginning, so it should appropriately conclude at the end. In the last two chapters in all the Bible, John is given a vision of what the new heaven and new earth will be like. He gives us many wonderful things to look forward to. One of them involves light—or the lack thereof. He writes:

> And the city has no need of sun or moon to shine on it, for the glory of God gives it light, and its lamp is the Lamb. By its light will the nations walk, and the kings of the earth will bring their glory into it, and its gates will never be shut by day… And night will be no more. They will need no light of lamp or sun, for the Lord God will be their light, and they will reign forever and ever. (Rev. 21:23-25, 22:5)

For now, we live in 'this present darkness' (Eph. 6:12). This world is full of darkness, both physical and spiritual. It abounds, it spreads, and sometimes it seems like the darkness is winning. Physical and spiritual darkness are connected. The deeds of spiritual darkness flourish in physical darkness, where they can be better hidden. Crime increases when the sun goes down. It is human nature to hide our sin and keep it secret. We need light to see, to walk, and to work. We also need it to expose and protect us from the forces and the deeds of darkness.

But there will be a day when darkness will be no more, and therefore lights will no longer be needed. The Lord, who dwells in unapproachable light (1 Tim. 6:16), is so radiant and so holy that darkness cannot exist in His presence. In the new earth, the Lord will be with us, ever present. 'And the name of the city from that time on shall be, *The Lord Is There*' (Eze. 48:35). So, as John tells us, lights will no longer be necessary. God Himself will radiate all the light we could ever need.

CHAPTER 13

A DESIRE TO SEE GOD

It was the most authentic, sincere prayer I have ever heard. When I was in college, I was discipling a young man by the name of Nick. One day in my dorm room, we were praying, as we always did before we studied the Bible together, and Nick said something in his prayer that I have never forgotten. He said, 'God, I don't want you right now. But I *want* to want you.' What hit me like a ton of bricks in that moment was the thought that this was exactly the kind of prayer God would want from His children. Nick didn't put on a facade of holiness, or try to fake feelings of love for God he didn't have. He just told God exactly what was on his heart.

I begin this chapter with Nick's prayer because seeing God starts with a desire to see Him. I know that might sound completely obvious, but without a desire to see God pushing us to seek Him more and more, nothing in this entire book will matter. Nick didn't feel the desire, but he had a desire to feel it. One litmus test for whether or not someone has genuinely been born again is if this desire or hunger for God (or at least a desire for the desire) is present in their hearts. Martyn Lloyd-Jones once wrote,

> The most vital question to ask about all who claim to be Christians is this: Have they a soul thirst for God? Do they long for this? Is there something about them that tells you

that they are always waiting for His next manifestation of Himself? Is their life centered on Him? Can they say with Paul that they forget everything in the past? Do they press forward more and more that they might know Him, and that the knowledge might increase, until eventually beyond death and the grave they may bask eternally in 'the sunshine of His face'?[1]

Similarly, John Piper writes, 'The strongest, most mature Christians I have ever met are the hungriest for God. It might seem that those who eat most would be least hungry. But that's not the way it works with an inexhaustible fountain, and an infinite feast, and a glorious Lord.'[2]

God Wants Us to Want Him

As you read through God's Word you will find the language of desire everywhere. It is not enough to obediently follow God's commands. We must do them with joy, from the heart. We must find our satisfaction in God, and Him alone. We must pursue Him. We see it in the words of the Apostles given directly to us. Paul *commands* us to 'Rejoice in the Lord' (Phil. 3:1, 4:4) and tells us that God loves it not just when we give, but when we do so cheerfully (2 Cor. 9:7). Peter commands us, 'Like newborn infants, *long* for the pure spiritual milk, that by it you may grow up into salvation' (1 Pet. 2:2, emphasis added).

Jesus tells us, 'Blessed are those who hunger and thirst for righteousness, for they shall be satisfied' (Matt. 5:6). He commands us to, '*seek* first the kingdom of God and his righteousness' (Matt. 6:33, emphasis added). Paul says to the Greeks in Acts 17 that God created humans 'that they should seek God' (Acts 17:27).

In the Old Testament, we read that David was a man after God's own heart (1 Sam. 13:14), which means not only that he had a heart like God's, but that he was *after* a heart like God's. He was pursuing a godly heart. This same David wrote beautiful poetry expressing his desire for the Lord. 'As a deer pants for flowing streams, so pants my soul for you, O God. My soul thirsts for God, for the

---

1. D. Martyn Lloyd-Jones, *God's Ultimate Purpose: An Exposition of Ephesians 1:1-23* (Grand Rapids: Baker, 1978), 349.

2. John Piper, *A Hunger for God: Desiring God Through Fasting and Prayer* (Wheaton: Crossway, 1997), 22-23.

living God. When shall I come and appear before God?' (Ps 42:1-2). 'O God, you are my God; earnestly I seek you; my soul thirsts for you; my flesh faints for you, as in a dry and weary land where there is no water' (Ps. 63:1).

In Isaiah, God spoke of people who, 'draw near with their mouth and honor me with their lips, while their hearts are far from me, and their fear of me is a commandment taught by men' (Is. 29:13). Notice that last phrase. They had a form of the fear of the Lord, but it was simply 'a commandment taught by men.' In other words, they went through the motions of what they thought the fear of the Lord should look like. But in their hearts, they did not truly fear Him. Jesus would later quote this to the Pharisees and scribes who hypocritically sacrificed the will of God for the sake of their own traditions (see Matthew 15:1-9).

This is but a small fraction of the multitude of passages that speak of the desire we should have for the Lord. God is clearly telling us that He expects His children to have a desire for Him, to long for Him, and to pursue Him. You cannot find a genuine believer in Scripture who does not also have this desire for God Himself.

What If I Don't Desire God?

For some, these examples will inspire and motivate them to pursue the Lord with a greater fervency. But others may experience discouragement. *It sounds as though Paul and Peter and David were just on fire for the Lord. What if I don't feel it? What if my desire for God simply is not there?* If this is you, perhaps one of the two following points will help.

First, you need to examine whether or not you have truly been born again. Without the Holy Spirit dwelling inside of you, this desire simply will not exist. An emotional spark may flare up for a short time, but it will not last. Unbelievers can even obey the commands of God outwardly without treasuring Him in their hearts. Have you truly given your life to Christ? The book of 1 John is a wonderful diagnostic tool for examining our status before God. John explicitly stated at the end of the book, 'I write these things to you who believe in the name of the Son of God, that you may know that you have eternal life' (1 John 5:13). Read through this short book and stop each time you notice John making a distinction between the person who knows God and the person who does not.

Another way to discern whether or not you have been born again is to talk with a mature believer who clearly knows and walks with God. This may be a pastor, an elder in your church, or another believer who has followed Christ for years. Actually, it would be wise to talk to more than one. Ask them to give you their honest assessment of your salvation. You may simply have unbiblical doubts, but on the other hand you may come to understand that you have never actually been born again in Christ. As we have seen previously, seeing God cannot happen until we come to God through Jesus and have our eyes opened by Him.

If you are confident that you are indeed a born-again believer, perhaps this second point will be beneficial. While God wants us to desire Him, and even commands it in Scripture, the fact remains we cannot manufacture desire for something. We cannot will ourselves to it. If I were to command you, *'Desire Jesus!'* that wouldn't really make any sense, would it? You would respond by saying, 'I'm sorry. I just don't!' It would be like my wife telling me that I should like cauliflower. Perhaps I should, but let me tell you, I don't! No amount of willpower or psyching myself up is going to make it taste good in my mouth. I simply don't like it.

But while we cannot manufacture desire within ourselves, it is possible to cultivate a desire. If your body is not accustomed to regular exercise, starting a regular workout program will feel awful at first. Initially your body is going to rebel against it. However, if over time you discipline yourself to do it regularly, it will slowly become easier. If you continue for long enough you will reach the point where you actually want to exercise, and you feel uneasy if you miss a day. I don't plan on trying it, but if I forced myself to eat cauliflower every day for a month, I suppose there is a decent chance I would begin to like it.

The same is true for spiritual disciplines such as Bible reading and prayer. J. I. Packer and Carolyn Nystrom wrote a book on prayer for which the subtitle is *Finding Our Way Through Duty to Delight*. That is a wonderful explanation of how to cultivate a godly desire. You begin by forcing yourself out of duty, but if you are consistent for long enough, you will become intrinsically motivated to do it. While we must stress that being born again, and having the Holy Spirit dwelling inside you is a prerequisite, desire for God can be cultivated through consistent spiritual disciplines, especially Bible reading and prayer.

At this point someone might ask, 'What is the difference between starting out with duty with the goal of delight versus outward obedience that God detests? If my heart is not in it, won't God be unhappy with me like He was with the Pharisees?'

The difference is essentially the heart behind Nick's prayer at the beginning of the chapter. The Pharisees performed their outward duties as a means of seeking their own glory, while the genuine believer practices spiritual disciplines out of duty hoping that one day it will lead to delight. She does not want God at the moment, but she *wants* to want Him. She is pursuing the desire. This makes all the difference.

It is also essential to remember that our desire for God and our fight against sin are directly related. Just as we may cultivate a desire for God, it is also possible to cultivate a desire for sin. The more you sin, the more you will desire it, and the less you will desire God. These desires are diametrically opposed to one another. When one goes up, the other goes down. Therefore, if we want to cultivate a desire for God, we must also be working hard to kill off sin in our lives by the power of the Spirit (Rom. 8:13). Much like our bodies and their desires for junk food or healthy nutrients, you will find that the desire that wins is the one that gets fed most consistently.

Pursuing at All Costs

Here is a crucial question we must ask ourselves in this pursuit: What if seeing God can only come through suffering or trials? Does our desire to see Him eclipse our desire to avoid those things? The reason this question matters so much is that history clearly shows us that those who see the Lord most intimately, and desire Him most fervently, had to come through suffering to reach that point.

In recent years I have greatly benefited from the sermons, books, and podcast episodes of a particular pastor. I remember multiple times thinking thoughts like, *'He knows Jesus so intimately! I wish I knew Jesus like that.'* It was only later that I realized that he spent a number of years going through intense suffering, stress, and emotional pain. Immediately I was struck that it was likely these trials were a major factor in his deep level of intimacy with Christ.

Just the other day I was speaking with a teenager who struggles with anxiety. She said that when she can't stop worrying, she prays constantly. I immediately realized it might be a way God is helping her to obey Paul's command in 1 Thessalonians 5:17: 'Pray without ceasing.' I have often asked God to help me to pray more. I had never considered that He might do it by putting me through a trial.

Paul himself only came to a deep dependence upon the grace of God through his thorn in the flesh. A thorn God refused to remove as a means of teaching Paul to depend on God and not himself for strength (see 2 Corinthians 12:7-10). For centuries, Christians have read Paul's letters and aspired to have eyes to see like Paul's. Yet Paul's sight was developed through intense suffering and trial, as he writes about in 2 Corinthians 11:16-33.

Consider Job's amazing encounter with God in Job 38–42. How many of us desire to have God speak directly to us like He did Job? Yet, as philosopher and theologian Vern Poythress writes,

> If we think we want to have an experience like Job's, we might first think about whether we really want the 'full package,' so to speak. For example, do we want to go through the suffering that Job experienced that led up to the climactic encounter with God? And even if we could avoid the suffering of Job, do we really want to be overwhelmed by encountering the infinite God as Job did? In reality, it is frightening.[3]

When God gave Isaiah that wonderful prophecy of Christ that became the suffering servant passage of Isaiah chapter 53, one of the lines reads as follows: 'Out of the anguish of his soul, he shall see and be satisfied' (Is. 53:11). Of course, this is specifically speaking of Christ and does not apply to us directly, but the principle behind it is a common experience. Suffering and anguish often produce a sight of God that could not be had otherwise, which results in a satisfaction in God that also could not be had otherwise. If we long to see and be satisfied (as we all should), we must realize that the path may take us through suffering. But take heart and strengthen your resolve. The end result is absolutely worth it.

---

3. Vern S. Poythress, *Theophany: A Biblical Theology of God's Appearing* (Wheaton: Crossway, 2018), 18.

A DESIRE TO SEE GOD

Do We Want God or His Gifts?

> Now there was a man in Jerusalem, whose name was Simeon, and this man was righteous and devout, waiting for the consolation of Israel, and the Holy Spirit was upon him. And it had been revealed to him by the Holy Spirit that he would not see death before he had seen the Lord's Christ. And he came in the Spirit into the temple, and when the parents brought in the child Jesus, to do for him according to the custom of the Law, he took him up in his arms and blessed God and said, 'Lord, now you are letting your servant depart in peace, according to your word; for my eyes have seen your salvation that you have prepared in the presence of all peoples, a light for revelation to the Gentiles, and for glory to your people Israel.' (Luke 2:25-32)

Simeon's brief appearance in Luke's gospel account might not seem like much at first glance, but his story holds a place of honor among the greatest saints in history because of his single-minded desire to see the Lord. Like David, Simeon desired 'one thing' (Ps. 27:4)—to see Jesus. Once he did, he essentially said, 'God, now I can die happy' (Luke 2:29)! For Simeon, seeing the Messiah was the end of it all. He didn't want Jesus as a means to some other desire, as so many in that day. He just wanted Jesus! Seeing Jesus was its own reward, not a means to something else.

Do you want God or do you want what He can give you? There's a big difference. Some people are desperate to see God, or to hear God speak audibly to them, so that others will think they are special. They long for others to come to them as the spiritual guru, the one who has a secret access to God that no one else does. Some want God because of the comfortable life they believe He will give them. Some want power, some knowledge, some influence. Some simply want God to heal their loved one.

One of my favorite characters in the Old Testament is Mephibosheth. In 2 Samuel 9, we read of how David, due to his close friendship with Jonathan, showed kindness to Mephibosheth as the only remaining descendent of Saul. Even though Mephibosheth was a lame beggar, David granted him a daily seat at the king's table, land, and thirty-five servants to work it and care for his every need. It is a wonderful picture of the undeserved grace each one of us has received from God.

But one of those servants was not very happy with the arrangement. His name was Ziba. When David's evil son Absalom tries to steal the throne, David flees out of town for fear of his life. Ziba comes to David's aid with supplies. When David asks Ziba why Mephibosheth didn't come too, Ziba lies and says he remained because he wanted Saul's line to re-take the throne. This could not be farther from the truth, for we learn later that Mephibosheth mourned David's absence every day until he returned. David responds to Ziba's lie by giving him all of the land he previously gave to Mephibosheth.

When David finally does return, he finds Mephibosheth and learns the truth. He says the land will be divided between him and Ziba. Mephibosheth replies by saying, 'Oh, let him take it all, since my lord the king has come safely home' (2 Sam. 19:30). Do you see? He doesn't care about the land. Mephibosheth did not love David because of what he could get from him. His delight was in David himself. His devotion to the king was complete and from the heart. Nothing could make him happier than seeing David return and take his rightful place on the throne. This is how we should love and desire God.

We do not desire God as a means to a happy life, or respect in the community, or an end to our struggles, or satisfying relationships. We may receive those blessings when we pursue God, or we may not. But at the most fundamental level, we desire God because we believe that He alone can satisfy the desires of our hearts. 'Delight yourself in the Lord, and he will give you the desires of your heart' (Ps. 37:4).

Seeing Requires Seeking

The natural expression of a desire for God is seeking Him. The Bible is full of examples, commandments, and encouragements to seek God. In Matthew 7:7, Jesus said, 'Seek and you will find.' Among other things, this means when we truly seek God, He will make sure we find Him. In one of my favorite promises in all of Scripture, God tells the Israelites, 'You will seek me and find me, when you seek me with all your heart' (Jer. 29:13; cf. Deut. 4:29 and 1 Chr. 28:9).

Isaiah tells us to 'Seek the Lord while he may be found; call upon him while he is near' (Is. 55:6). In other words, do not put off seeking the Lord until later in your life. There are some who, through continually hardening their heart against the will of God, find that in the end they no longer have the ability to turn to the Lord. For certain, when Christ returns it will be too late for all who have put off seeking the Lord. So, seek Him while you still can. Seek Him while He may be found.

David, who is perhaps our best model of seeking the Lord other than Jesus, tells us to 'Seek the Lord and his strength; seek his presence continually!' (1 Chr. 16:11). There are so many beautiful examples throughout Christian history of those who were consumed by seeking God's presence. I think of Brother Lawrence and *The Practice of the Presence of God*, who literally tried to keep God at the forefront of his mind every waking minute of his days.

And I think of A. W. Tozer, and his classic book *The Pursuit of God*, which has influenced my writing and my walk with God in so many ways. Tozer ends each chapter with a prayer. The prayers alone are worth the price of the book. I conclude this chapter with his wonderfully fitting prayer from the chapter entitled 'Following Hard After God':

> O God, I have tasted Thy goodness, and it has both satisfied me and made me thirsty for more. I am painfully conscious of my need of further grace. I am ashamed of my lack of desire. O God, the Triune God, I want to want Thee; I long to be filled with longing; I thirst to be made more thirsty still. Show me Thy glory, I pray Thee, that so I may know Thee indeed. Begin in mercy a new work of love within me. Say to my soul, 'Rise up, my love, my fair one, and come away.' Then give me grace to rise and follow Thee up from this misty lowland where I have wandered so long. In Jesus' Name, Amen.[4]

---

4. A. W. Tozer, *The Pursuit of God* (Bloomington: Bethany House, 2013), 28.

CHAPTER 14

THE GAZE OF THE SOUL

A.W. Tozer knew God more deeply and saw God more clearly than just about any person I am aware of. If you read *The Pursuit of God*, you will be immediately struck by the evidence that this was a man who pursued God with everything he had, and yet was always thirsty for more. He treasured knowing and experiencing God above all things. Tozer certainly had his flaws,[1] but no one can deny that his heart burned and yearned for God more intensely than most.

I swiped the title of this chapter from his own chapter seven in *The Pursuit of God*. Tozer depicts a man who reads through the Bible for the very first time, with no prior knowledge at all, and comes to understand that this thing called 'faith' must be absolutely essential to the Christian life. But what is it? How would you go about defining it? The closest thing to a definition of faith in the Bible is Hebrews 11:1, but even there, it is describing what faith is in action, not what it is *in essence*.

---

1.   Lyle Dorsett, in his excellent biography, *A Passion for God: The Spiritual Journey of A. W. Tozer* (Chicago: Moody Publishers, 2008), chronicles Tozer's consistent neglect of his wife and children, for example.

Looking and Believing

Tozer refers back to Moses' bronze serpent in Numbers 21. The people grumbled and complained against God, and said they wanted to go back to Egypt. So, God sent deadly serpents among their camp and they began biting the people. The Israelites were frightened, and many were dying. Moses pleaded with the Lord on their behalf, and God gave Moses a way for the people to be saved. He told Moses to fashion a serpent made of bronze, to set it up on a pole in a high, visible place, and everyone who looked upon the serpent would live.

Thousands of years later, Jesus would reveal to Nicodemus that this serpent was an Old Testament foreshadowing of His own death on the cross. 'And as Moses lifted up the serpent in the wilderness, so must the Son of Man be lifted up, that whoever believes in him may have eternal life' (John 3:14-15).

So, Tozer writes,

> Our plain man in reading this would make an important discovery. He would notice that "look" and "believe" were synonymous terms. "Looking" on the Old Testament serpent is identical with "believing" on the New Testament Christ. That is, the looking and the believing are the same thing. And he would understand that while Israel looked with their external eyes, believing is done with the heart. I think he would conclude that faith is the gaze of a soul upon a saving God.[2]

That last sentence is the ultimate point Tozer is driving at in his chapter, and also the point I am driving at in mine here. Seeing God with the eyes of our hearts is the very essence of faith. We must look to God by looking to Jesus (Heb. 12:2) for the initial grace of salvation, and we must continue to look to Him for the sustained grace of perseverance. In other words, gazing at God through Christ is what saves us, and it is also what keeps us saved.

Tozer again writes, 'From all this we learn that faith is not a once-done act, but a continuous gaze of the heart at the Triune God. Believing, then, is directing the heart's attention to Jesus. It is lifting the mind to "behold the Lamb of God," and never ceasing that beholding for the rest of our lives.'[3]

---

2. Tozer, *The Pursuit of God*, 82.
3. Ibid., 83.

This is especially helpful when we encounter those who 'believe' that Jesus existed, died on the cross, and rose from the dead, and are therefore convinced they are saved. Saving faith is about more than assent to the facts of history. Even Satan and his demons accept these facts about Christ, but this does not save them (Jas. 2:19). When Jesus says in John 3:16 that 'whoever believes in him shall not perish but have eternal life,' He means this gaze of the soul.

The Impossible Made Easy

The Bible is always telling us to do what cannot be done. Jesus tells us to 'Be perfect' (Matt. 5:48). Paul tells us to know what surpasses knowledge (Eph. 3:19). You must be born again (John 3:3). And, in this book, we have examined how we must see this God whom no one has ever seen, nor can see, and if you were to see Him you would die. It is no wonder some throw their hands up in frustration and say, 'I will never live up to His standards! Maybe some other people are strong enough, smart enough, and have enough will-power, but normal folks like me are left on the outside looking in.'

But the beauty of knowing God is that, while we will never plumb the depths of the riches and wisdom and knowledge of God (Rom. 11:33), God has made faith and salvation simple enough that anyone can do it. In fact, it's so simple, the smartest and most self-disciplined will often have a more difficult time of it.

Here is Tozer again:

> Now, if faith is the gaze of the heart at God, and if this gaze is but the raising of the inward eyes to meet the all-seeing eyes of God, then it follows that it is one of the easiest things possible to do. It would be like God to make the most vital thing easy and place it within the range of possibility for the weakest and poorest of us.[4]

The more I come to know God, the more I find myself saying those words, '*It would be just like God to do that*,' in my everyday conversations. As we grow deeper and more intimate in our relationship with Him, we come to know His heart, His values, and even, I think, His tendencies. Therefore, our discernment grows as well. As you mature in Christ, you will find that some things you hear simply don't smell right spiritually. Your spiritual senses will

---

4. Ibid., 86.

throw up red flags. But at other times, as someone is sharing with you about their life, you will find yourself thinking or saying, '*That sounds just like something God would do.*'

God has made the most vital thing—faith—easy and placed it on the lowest shelf, easily accessible to any who would reach for it. To flesh this out, Tozer highlights three ways that faith is not restricted to the spiritual elite, but is easily accessible to all. First, you don't need special equipment or skills. Those who are weak and poor can take encouragement from the fact that while certain people may have a built-in advantage over them in finances, power, intellect, or worldly opportunity, there is no such thing when it comes to faith. 'Blessed are the poor in spirit... blessed are the meek... blessed are those who are persecuted.'

When it comes to seeing God, the chairman of the elders has no inherent advantage over the teenage girl in the pews. The preacher has no inherent advantage over the nursery volunteer. And the wealthy man seen as a pillar in his community has no inherent advantage over the single mom living paycheck to paycheck.

Second, Tozer notes that this seeing/believing/looking can be done at any time. We do not have to wait for special days of the Christian calendar to gaze upon the beauty and glory of God. We are no closer to God on Easter Sunday than we are on Saturday, August 3 or Monday, October 4.[5] You have just as much access at this moment as you do on Sunday during the worship service.

Third, and finally, just as time does not matter, neither does place. Since seeing God happens in our inner being, with the eyes of our hearts, you can do it from anywhere. I may never be able to make a trip to the Holy Land, and walk where Jesus walked. But it makes no difference. I can know and see God just as well right here in Columbia, KY. You don't need to drive to the church building to pray fervently and seek the Lord. Get on your knees right there in your living room or bedroom. As Christ said to the Samaritan woman, a time is now here when we are not required to be in this temple or on that mountain to worship the Father. True worshipers can worship anywhere, in spirit and in truth. Brother Lawrence, in that wonderful book *The Practice of the Presence of God*, noted how he

---

5. Ibid., 86.

could experience the deep and overflowing presence of God while cooking eggs or gathering straw or any other daily duty.[6]

So, we find that this impossible task of seeing the unseen God is mysterious and unnatural, and yet it is extraordinarily simple and accessible at the same time. With God, the impossible becomes easy.

Developing and Training Our Inner Eyes

While it may be accessible and simple, this inner seeing does not come naturally to us. Therefore, we must grow into it. Like a seldom used muscle that is all of a sudden much needed because of a new job or a new activity, we must develop and train the eyes of our hearts to see or perceive God more regularly. The goal is not a glimpse here and a glimpse there, but a consistent awareness of His goodness, His glory, and His presence. The abiding joy that comes from this kind of lifestyle is absolutely priceless.

For most of us, our inner gaze is on the world and the things in the world by default. Through discipline and focus we can wrench it away from the world and onto God for a short time, but then, like a screen door on a spring, it snaps back to its default position. However, it is possible, over time, to train the eyes of our hearts to do the exact opposite. If we walk with the Lord, and gaze at His glory enough, slowly, probably imperceptibly, over the course of years and years, our default will change. Instead of having to wrench our inner eyes away from the world for a moment before they snap back, the world will actually become the momentary distraction. They will snap back to God.

This may sound impossible to those of us who have only walked with Christ for a small portion of our lives, but there are plenty of believers who experience this. Some never even take a step back to recognize it, which is probably just as well. The truly humble do not waste time analyzing their own virtues. Tozer writes, 'Many have found the secret of which I speak and, without much thought to what is going on within them, constantly practice this habit of inwardly gazing upon God. They know that something inside their hearts sees God.'[7]

Perhaps this is what Christ means when He says 'abide in me.' The consistent inner sight of God, of His goodness and His glory,

---

6. Lawrence, *The Practice of the Presence of God*, Kindle loc. 434.
7. Tozer, *Pursuit*, 87.

produces a settled and steady joy that the cares of this world cannot touch. Just the other day I was talking to a man who seems to live this way and he told me that while the chaos in the world seems to grow by the day, he has an inner peace that just does not leave. He could hardly explain it. Then he said, 'I guess that's why Paul calls it the peace that passes understanding.' Yes and amen.

CHAPTER 15

YOU MUST WORK HARD TO SEE GOD

There was once a very wise and respected professor who was approached by a student curious about scientific observation. 'Very well,' said the professor, taking out a huge jar. 'Take this fish and look at it. Eventually I'll test you.' The student sat down and started looking at the fish. After about ten minutes he thought he saw everything there was to be seen. He looked for the professor but he was nowhere to be found. So, the student kept looking at the fish. Thirty minutes passed. An hour. Two hours.

Finally, the professor returned. 'What have you observed?' The student rehearsed it all. The fleshy lips, the lidless eyes, the shimmering scales, the lateral line, the spinous fin, the forked tail. The professor seemed disappointed. 'You haven't looked very carefully. You haven't even seen some of the most obvious features. Keep looking.'

The student wanted nothing more to do with the fish. He was miserable. But he wanted to please the professor. So, he kept looking. Slowly he discovered one new feature after another. Soon time began to fly by as the student observed that fish. He discovered all kinds of things he'd never noticed before. He realized just how right the professor had been. After an hour the professor returned to a new list. 'That's good. But that's not all. Go on. Keep looking.'

And so, for three long days he put that fish before the student's eyes, forbidding him to study anything else, repeating the same chorus each time. 'Look... look... look.'[1]

Just like the student who had to look, and look, and keep looking (and keep focusing!) on that fish, seeing God does not simply happen to us. We must give it time, attention, and effort. We must pursue it with everything we have. 'You will seek me and find me, when you seek me with all your heart' (Jer. 29:13).

Seeing God is an undeserved gift of His grace, but that does not mean effort plays no part in it. This takes hard work. Grace-infused, Spirit-powered work. But don't despair! For those who desire God above all else, the work is not burdensome. In fact, most of the time it will not feel like work. Yet it is work all the same.

Two Biblical Examples

Consider two men who had to work hard to see Jesus. The first is Zacchaeus (see Luke 19:1-10), who had two large obstacles, or disadvantages, to overcome in his quest to catch a glimpse of Christ. First, he was a chief tax collector and was rich. He hired himself out to the Romans to collect their exorbitant taxes from the Jews. His wealth and comfort were a direct result of the suffering of his own people. He would have been considered a traitor. Think of a Jewish person during World War 2, passing information along to the Nazis about where his fellow Jews were hiding out. This meant Zacchaeus wasn't getting any help from the people.

Not only that, he was also a considerably short man. So, on the day he was trying to see Jesus in a crowd full of others who wanted to do the same, he was out of luck. He couldn't see over anyone, and no one was about to give up their spot for a traitor. The only way to see Jesus on that day was to scamper up a tree, like a little kid. Now, I don't know about you, but for me the prospect of climbing a tree as an adult is much, much different than doing it as a kid. I would have to be desperate to attempt something like that now

---

1. Desiring God, 'Keep Looking: The Life Changing Secret to Reading the Bible,' YouTube Video, 2:56, April 25, 2017, https://www.youtube.com/watch?v=KEP3s53VD4c.

(and I'm only thirty-six!). Not only that, but in the midst of a crowd, a grown man like me in a tree would attract all kinds of weird looks and probably a few words of ridicule.

This tells us something of Zacchaeus' strong desire to see Jesus. He was willing to do whatever it took. He did not give up after no one would let him through to see. He did not allow the prospect of ridicule to stop him from climbing a tree like a child. Have we not experienced this same principle in our own lives? If we want something bad enough, we will make sacrifices and overcome obstacles to get it. We will find a way because we must.

Next, consider the paralyzed man in Mark 2. The crowd that had gathered at this house was so large, there was simply no more room to get anyone close to Jesus, especially not a paralyzed man who had to be carried on a mat. But like Zacchaeus, those obstacles were not enough to stop this man and his loyal friends. Their desire for Jesus was too great. So, they carried him up on the roof and proceeded to rip a hole in it, even though it was not their house! Yet, because of their relentless pursuit of Jesus, the paralyzed man walked home that day, carrying his own mat.

This quest to see God will not be easy. It will not come to those who passively wait. It will take work, and risk, and even the willingness to be scorned by others. But the reward is worth all of it, and more. If we seek Him with all our heart, He will make sure we find Him, and when you find God—when you see Him—it never disappoints.

The Means of Our Pursuit

Our quest to see the Lord will likely not involve pushing through a crowd, or climbing a tree, or a roof. It's a pursuit to see what cannot be seen. It is much the same principle as when Paul tells us that the battle we are fighting cannot be fought against flesh and blood, with worldly weapons (see Ephesians 6:10-18). We are pursuing a spiritual sight with the eyes of our hearts. This sight comes through means such as the hard work of consistent Bible study.

Are you willing to study your Bible to see the glory of God? If not, you will never see more than a dim, fleeting glance. As we saw in chapter six, the primary way God shows us His glory is through His Word. The harder we work to study and understand it, the more of His glory we will see. Are you willing to put in the work?

Are you willing to study it regularly? To carve out time in your daily schedule for it, sometimes sacrificing things you enjoy such as television, sleep, or productivity? Are you willing to do it when your mind is most alert? To devote your best hours to the pursuit of seeing God? Are you willing to invest money into this pursuit? For tools that will help you study the Bible better? What could be a better use of your financial resources? Are you willing to study *all of Scripture*, and not just the easier parts, or the parts you enjoy most? Otherwise you may get a partial view of God, one that is not accurate or well-rounded.

Another means of pursuing the sight of God is fasting. John Piper's excellent book on fasting is fittingly titled *A Hunger for God*. Fasting is a way of saying to God, *I need you more than I need food*. Or we might say, *I need to see you and be satisfied in you more than I need to eat and be satisfied in food*. As Job said, 'I have cherished the words of his mouth more than my portion of food' (Job 23:12). In His wisdom and providence, God has given us the gift of fasting for various purposes. We may fast to intensely petition God on a certain prayer request. We may fast to seek discernment of the Lord's will in an important decision. In the Bible there are some who fasted as an expression of sadness and lament before the Lord.

But one of the most important purposes for fasting is increased intimacy with God. For whatever reason, God has ordained that going without food for certain periods of time heightens our spiritual senses and connects us to Him in a way we do not experience in the normal course of everyday life. I can attest to this from my own experience. While the lack of food will increase your feelings of weakness, it will also increase your sense of the Lord's presence. Perhaps the heightened awareness of weakness is the whole point, just as Paul learned to depend on God's strength through weakness (see 2 Cor. 12:7-10). Through fasting, God opens the eyes of our hearts just a bit more. Fasting clears away a fog that blurs our spiritual vision.

In fact, all the spiritual disciplines are means by which we pursue a greater sight of God and His glory. Through disciplines such as Bible reading, fasting, Scripture memory and meditation, confession, stewardship, evangelism, worship, silence and solitude, and others, we are training the eyes of our hearts to see God as an athlete trains his body. We must never think of them as a means of manipulating God, or forcing Him to show Himself, but rather through them we place ourselves nearer to Him, so that He may work on our hearts, and so that we may 'taste and see that the Lord is good. (Ps. 34:8).[2]

Physical, Not Just Spiritual

While the fight to see God is a spiritual one, we cannot discount how much our physical condition affects it. Fasting is one example of a physical act that is meant to produce a spiritual result. Our bodies, minds, and spirits are inherently connected. What happens to one impacts the others. Therefore, even in the quest to see God with spiritual sight, there is a physical aspect. The condition of our bodies matters.

We have all likely experienced the connection between our bodies and our minds. When we are sick our minds don't work as effectively. For me, when I eat a heavy lunch, I have a much harder time doing mental work effectively for the rest of the afternoon. On the other hand, when I have a light lunch, my brain works better.

I think we would all agree that our minds are essential in the pursuit of seeing God. Paul tells Timothy to '*Think* over what I say, for the Lord will give you understanding in everything' (2 Tim.2:7, emphasis added). In other words, use your brain to seek the Lord. If our brains are essential tools in knowing and seeing God, and if it is true that the condition of our bodies affects the ability of our minds, it follows that the condition of our bodies is an important factor in our pursuit to see God.

Jonathan Edwards once wrote,

> By a sparingness in diet, and eating as much as may be what is light and easy of digestion, I shall doubtless be able to think more clearly, and shall gain time; 1. By lengthening out my life; 2. Shall need less time for digestion, after meals; 3. Shall be able to study more closely, without injury to my health; 4. Shall need less time for sleep; 5. Shall more seldom be troubled with the head-ache.[3]

Now, we must be careful not to be legalistic here. There is a time for enjoying a cheeseburger and fries to the glory of God. But Edwards

2. In my opinion, the best book on spiritual disciplines is: Donald Whitney, *Spiritual Disciplines for the Christian Life*, (Colorado Springs: by NavPress, 2014).

3. Jonathan Edwards, *The Works of Jonathan Edwards: Volume One* (Carlisle: Banner of Truth, 1974), 35.

makes an important point about diet and care for the body and mind. Specifically, his example should convince us that many Christians have not allowed the gospel and the pursuit of seeing God to infect and reform their eating and exercise habits. This is not to say that every Christian needs to be in peak physical shape, but I think it does highlight the fact that if we do not practice self-restraint and discipline in our physical lives, we will typically be preventing ourselves from a deeper level of knowledge of and communion with God. It is an error characteristic of our times to think the body and the spirit have no connection, and therefore it does not matter how we treat our bodies.

Martin Lloyd-Jones, in his classic work *Spiritual Depression*, wrote:

> You cannot isolate the spiritual from the physical for we are body, mind and spirit. The greatest and the best Christians when they are physically weak are more prone to an attack of spiritual depression than at any other time and there are great illustrations of this in the Scriptures.[4]

This carries even more weight when we consider that Lloyd-Jones spent the first part of his adult life working as an acclaimed doctor in England. During those years he gained renown for his skills in diagnosing ailments and disease, as well as treating the whole person, not just the patient's physical symptoms.

The Choice Between What Is Great, and What Is Easy

In the last chapter, we saw A. W. Tozer's claim that God has made faith—seeing God with the eyes of our hearts—easy. By this, he did not mean that it requires no effort, but rather that God has made it *accessible* to all. In this chapter, we have found that while God may reveal Himself to the hearts of anyone at any time, seeing God is typically the result of a disciplined and consistent effort. This is not self-reliant will power, but grace-infused and Spirit-fueled hard work. Author and preacher Tim Keller, in his book on prayer, said, 'I can think of nothing great that is also easy.'[5] True for prayer. True for seeing God. But is not beholding the glory of God worth every effort?

---

4. Lloyd-Jones, *Spiritual Depression*, 19.

5. Timothy Keller, *Prayer: Experiencing Awe and Intimacy with God* (New York: Penguin, 2014), Kindle loc. 390.

In our pursuit to see God we will discipline our bodies (1 Cor. 9:27), we will think hard with our minds (2 Tim. 2:7), we will practice spiritual habits that lead us closer to God, and we will read, read, and read God's Word until we can read no more. Do you want to see God no matter what it takes? If you do, you will. 'You will seek me and find me when you seek me with all your heart' (Jer. 29:13).

To paraphrase one of the great lines from literature… there will be a time when we must choose between what is great, and what is easy. What will you choose? Will you settle for what pastor and author Wilbur Rees called '$3.00 Worth of God'? Or will you refuse to be satisfied, to put in the time and the energy and the sacrifice, to get a glimpse of His glory?

I would like to buy $3 worth of God, please.

Not enough to explode my soul or disturb my sleep, but just enough to equal a cup of warm milk

or a snooze in the sunshine.

I don't want enough of God to make me love a black man or pick beets with a migrant.

I want ecstasy, not transformation.

I want warmth of the womb, not a new birth.

I want a pound of the Eternal in a paper sack.

I would like to buy $3 worth of God, please.[6]

---

6.   Wilber E. Rees, *$3.00 Worth of God* (King of Prussia: Judson, 1971), 5.

CHAPTER 16

LOOKING FORWARD TO THE REWARD

On February 4, 1555, John Rogers was burned at the stake in London, England by the order of Queen Mary I. You might know her by her nickname, *Bloody Mary*. Rogers was executed for the crimes of denying the authority of the church of Rome, and for claiming that the bread and wine of communion did not actually transform into the body and blood of Jesus. J. C. Ryle recounts the day of his death:

> On the morning of his martyrdom he was roused hastily in his cell in Newgate, and hardly allowed time to dress himself. He was then led forth to Smithfield on foot, within sight of the Church of St. Sepulchre, where he had preached, and through the streets of the parish where he had done the work of a pastor. By the wayside stood his wife and ten children (one a baby) whom Bishop Bonnet, in his diabolical cruelty, had flatly refused him leave to see in prison. He just saw them, but was hardly allowed to stop, and then walked on calmly to the stake, repeating the 51st Psalm. An immense crowd lined the street, and filled every available spot in Smithfield. Up to that day men could not tell how English Reformers would behave in the face of death, and could hardly believe that Prebendaries and Dignitaries would actually give their bodies to be burned

for their religion. But when they saw John Rogers, the first martyr, walking steadily and unflinchingly into a fiery grave, the enthusiasm of the crowd knew no bounds. They rent the air with thunders of applause. Even Noailles, the French Ambassador, wrote home a description of the scene, and said that Rogers went to death 'as if he was walking to his wedding'.[1]

Ryle goes on to tell of the accounts of others during that time who faced their martyrdom with peace, joy, and confidence. For example, John Bradford, who was burned for his faith in that same year, just before his execution, kissed his stake, then turned to another young man next to him facing the same sentence, and said, 'Be of good comfort brother, for we shall have a merry supper with the Lord this night!'[2] In 1543, Helen Starke was sentenced to be put in a sack and drowned for her faith in Christ. Her husband was also sentenced to be killed on the same day in a different fashion. They had just had a newborn baby. Just before her execution by drowning she calmly said to her husband, 'Husband, rejoice, for we have lived together many joyful days, but this day, on which we must die, ought to be most joyful unto us both, for we must have joy forever. Therefore, I will not bid you good night, for we shall suddenly meet with joy in the kingdom of Heaven.'[3]

How could each of these men and women have had such peace and confidence facing down a horrific death? The explanation is clear from their final recorded words and deeds. They were looking forward to their eternal reward.

Hebrews 11 and the Eyes of Faith

In that great chapter recounting the heroes of faith, Hebrews 11, we find that the confident faith of so many Old Testament saints was a result of a future-oriented spiritual sight. They were looking past this present life to what awaits those who remain faithful to God. For example, the author begins the chapter by writing, 'Now faith

---

1. J. C. Ryle, *Five English Reformers* (Carlisle: Banner of Truth, 1960), Kindle loc. 131.

2. Ibid., Kindle loc. 234.

3. Together for the Gospel (T4G), 'Martyrdom and Mission Why Reformers Died In Their Day, How We Must Live In Ours,' YouTube Video, 57:37, May 27, 2016, https://www.youtube.com/watch?v=RJ15kEmneM0&t=3333s.

is the assurance of things hoped for, the conviction of things not seen' (Heb. 11:1). In other words, faith is about seeing with spiritual eyes what cannot be seen with physical eyes, and then placing your confident trust in it. We see this forward-looking spiritual sight in the faith of Noah, who believed God's warning 'concerning events yet unseen' (verse 7), and in Abraham, whose faith was the result of '*looking forward* to the city that has foundations, whose designer and builder is God' (verse 10, emphasis added).

We also see both Isaac and Jacob commended for their forward-looking faith (verses 20-21). Both were physically blind in their old age, but pronounced future blessings on their children and grandchildren through a spiritual sight that could only have been given by God. It might confuse us at first why Isaac is commended for having blessed his boys in the way he did. After all, his blessings on Jacob and Esau were the result of Jacob's deception. Isaac was duped into giving Jacob the blessing of the eldest son as a result of his physical blindness. But God, in His perfect wisdom, used the physical blindness to show off His grace and glory. In the end, the blessings went to each son exactly as the Lord intended, and Isaac is rightly commended as one who, though physically blind, received a spiritual sight of the future by faith, and thus prophesied over his boys.

Then we immediately read of Jacob, the selfish deceiver whose heart was slowly melted, over the course of his life, by the undeserved grace of God. In his last days, also being physically blind (or at least very near to it[4]), he marvels at God's goodness because he has received Joseph back after years of having thought he was dead, and not only this, but he now has two grandsons as well! As Joseph places the two boys before Jacob to receive his blessing, he puts Manasseh, the older, in front of Jacob's right hand, the proper place for Jacob to bestow the blessing of the eldest son. Ephraim is placed before Jacob's left hand. But Jacob, in faith, not being able to see which boy is in front of him, crosses his hands, and lays his right on the younger, and his left on the older, and blesses the boys accordingly. When Joseph tries to correct him, Jacob says, 'I know, my son, I know' (Heb. 11:19). In a beautiful turn of events, Jacob has been so humbled by the grace of God, that he now intentionally

---

4. 'Now the eyes of Israel were dim with age, so that he could not see' (Gen. 48:10).

reverses the blessings in the same way that Isaac unintentionally did to him. He now sees with the eyes of his heart what he could not see for most of his life with his physical eyes. This is apparently such an act of faith that it is now forever what Jacob is remembered for in the great chapter of the heroes of faith.

This forward-looking spiritual sight is perhaps most clearly displayed in the verses that follow. The author goes on to say,

> These all died in faith, not having received the things promised, but having seen them and greeted them from afar, and having acknowledged that they were strangers and exiles on the earth. For people who speak thus make it clear that they are seeking a homeland. If they had been thinking of that land from which they had gone out, they would have had opportunity to return. But as it is, they desire a better country, that is, a heavenly one. Therefore God is not ashamed to be called their God, for he has prepared for them a city... Some were tortured, refusing to accept release, so that they might rise again to a better life... And all these, though commended through their faith, did not receive what was promised, since God had provided something better for us, that apart from us they should not be made perfect. (Heb. 11:13-16, 35, 39-40)

They did not receive what was promised—at least not in their lifetimes—but they lived convinced that they would receive it upon their death. Some, it says, refused release from torture. Why? Because much like John Rogers, John Bradford, and Helen Starke, they knew they were moments away from receiving their reward. How foolish would it have been to come so close, and then to throw it all away? A few more moments of torture for the reward of the presence of Christ, eternal bliss, and paradise beyond belief? I'll take that deal every time.

One of the verses that sparked the idea for this book is found in Hebrews 11:27, which says Moses 'persevered because he saw him who is invisible' (Heb. 11:27, NIV84). This entire book is essentially my best answer to the question, *How can we, like Moses, see Him who is invisible?* I should say, the answer does not come from me, but from God's Word. Nevertheless, in the verse immediately preceding that one, we read that Moses 'considered the reproach of Christ greater wealth than the treasures of Egypt, *for he was looking to the reward*' (Heb. 11:26, emphasis added). What gave Moses the confidence to sacrifice life in the palace and to identify himself with poor and horribly mistreated slaves? Looking forward to the reward. The same spiritual sight that allowed him to see the invisible God, also allowed him to perceive what awaited him on the other side of death, and thus gave him the power to act for God in faith.

One of the implications of this for us today is that an essential element of our faith must be looking forward to the reward that awaits us on the other side of death if we remain faithful to Christ. This is the only way we can confidently face down the suffering that life inevitably brings, or the persecution that walking with Christ inevitably brings. Ray Ortlund writes, 'The great thing right now about your future is this. Any time at all, by faith, you can go there in your mind. Paint the picture for the eyes of your heart. You'll have fresh energy for living nobly amid the ruins of this tragic world. You'll need it. But you'll have it—always.'[5]

Only with a future-oriented spiritual sight can we say, with Paul, 'For I consider that the sufferings of this present time are not worth comparing with the glory that is to be revealed to us... For in this hope we were saved. Now hope that is seen is not hope. For who hopes for what he sees?' (Rom. 8:18, 24). 'We walk by faith, not by sight' (2 Cor. 5:7).

The Danger of Comfort

We should note the fundamental connection between looking forward to our eternal reward and the suffering we experience in this life. These two go hand-in-hand. It is true that the more we look forward to our future reward, the greater our strength to face suffering here and now. But it is also true that, for those who have this true hope of faith, the more suffering they experience, the more frequently they look forward to their reward on the other side of death. This means that seasons of comfort present a spiritual danger to us. The more comfortable, or *at home*, we are in this world, the less time we will spend looking forward to the reward.

Matthew Westerholm, professor of Church Music and Worship at Southern Baptist Theological Seminary, has insightfully observed that 'American evangelical churches aren't singing about heaven as

---

5. Ray Ortlund, *The Death of Porn: Men of Integrity Building a World of Nobility* (Wheaton: Crossway, 2021), 66.

often or as well as they used to.'[6] He bases this claim on a recent research project comparing the most commonly sung congregational songs in the US from the years 2000 to 2015 with the most commonly published congregational songs in the US from 1737 to 1960. One of his most interesting conclusions: 'the topic of heaven, which once was frequently and richly sung about, has now all but disappeared.'[7]

This is not surprising considering the significant advancement in recent decades of services, technology, health care, and amenities aimed at making life easier. As our comfort has increased, our songs that look forward to heaven have decreased. A study of African-American spirituals and hymns produced during the years of American slavery will reveal a consistent future-oriented focus on heaven, the place where believers will finally be free of injustice, oppression, and sadness.

When we experience trials and suffering, we can face them with hope if we look forward to our reward. But when we find ourselves in seasons of comfort, we must discipline ourselves to look forward because it will not come naturally. This is yet another reason we must be regularly reading and hearing God's Word. A steady and balanced diet of all Scripture will consistently bring our minds back to our homeland (Heb. 11:14), 'the city that has foundations, whose designer and builder is God' (Heb. 11:10).

A Believer's Last Moments Before Death

In Acts 7 we read the account of the martyrdom of Stephen. After a lengthy speech about God's dealings with the Israelites, Stephen condemns the elders, the scribes, and others there for resisting the Holy Spirit and the message of the gospel of Christ. Then we read this:

> Now when they heard these things they were enraged, and they ground their teeth at him. But he, full of the Holy Spirit, gazed into heaven and saw the glory of God, and Jesus standing at the right hand of God. And he said, 'Behold, I see the heavens opened, and the Son of Man

6. Matthew Westerholm, 'The Church Should Sing for Heaven's Sake: When and Why We Stopped Singing about Heaven, and How to Start Again,' *9Marks*, Dec. 22, 2020, https://www.9marks.org/article/the-church-should-sing-for-heavens-sake-when-and-why-we-stopped-singing-about-heaven-and-how-to-start-again/.

7. Ibid.

standing at the right hand of God.' But they cried out with a loud voice and stopped their ears and rushed together at him. Then they cast him out of the city and stoned him. And the witnesses laid down their garments at the feet of a young man named Saul. And as they were stoning Stephen, he called out, 'Lord Jesus, receive my spirit.' And falling to his knees he cried out with a loud voice, 'Lord, do not hold this sin against them.' And when he had said this, he fell asleep. (Acts 7:54-60)

Just before he was stoned to death God gave Stephen a vision of His glory and of Jesus standing at His right hand. I am convinced one of the reasons God allowed Stephen to see this was to strengthen and comfort him so he could endure the gruesome and agonizingly painful death he was about to experience. God was helping Stephen to die.

Perhaps you have heard stories of how Christians, in their dying moments, will suddenly speak of seeing the glory of God or of heaven with their waking eyes. I remember an elder in the church where I grew up, telling of the last moments of an elderly man who was a church member and a strong believer. Just before his last breath he told those in the room, 'I see home.' Charles Spurgeon, one of the most well-known preachers in church history, would often comment how he frequently experienced this as he was in the room with believers in their dying moments. In one sermon he said,

> Oh, what brave things do they tell of the heavenly world! What glorious speeches do they make! To some of them the veil has been thrown back, and they have spoken of things not seen as yet. They have almost declared things which it were not lawful for men to utter, and, therefore, their speech has been broken, and mysterious, like dark sayings upon a harp. We could hardly make out all they said, but we gathered that they were overwhelmed with glory, that they were confounded with unutterable bliss, that they had seen and fain would tell but must not, they had heard and fain would repeat but could not. 'Did you not see the glory?' they have said.[8]

---

8. Charles Spurgeon, 'Precious Deaths,' *Metropolitan Tabernacle Pulpit volume 18*, Feb. 18, 1872, https://www.spurgeon.org/resource-library/sermons/precious-deaths/#flipbook/.

Of course, we cannot objectively verify these visions. However, Stephen's dying moments, along with the testimony of so many who have been present during the passing of believers, suggest to us that God may very well often give His dying saints a brief glimpse of His glory, or the glories of what awaits them, to shepherd them through the passage of death. 'Precious in the sight of the Lord is the death of his saints' (Ps. 116:15). Also, precious is the Lord in the sight of His dying saints.

Seeing Now Prepares Us for Seeing Then

The reward we are looking forward to is more than simply an eternal home without pain or sadness. We will see God and behold His glory. Yes, we can see Him now, but it is a veiled form only accessed by the eyes of our hearts. One day we will see Him face to face. Remember what God said to Moses on Mount Sinai after Moses asked to see His glory? 'You cannot see my face, for man shall not see me and live' (Ex. 33:20). Yet at the very end of the Bible, the angel speaks to the Apostle John of eternal life and says, *'They will see his face*, and his name will be on their foreheads' (Rev. 22:4, emphasis added).

Here it is important to remember, God does not literally have a face. He is an uncreated spirit. Any face He presents to human beings on earth, or to those in heaven, is a theophany, a manifestation of Himself in a form that can be seen. His unveiled, pure glory is invisible (1 Tim. 1:17, 6:16). The most helpful explanation I have found of this principle comes from Jack Cottrell, when he writes,

> Just as God is naturally invisible to the material realm because he is spirit, so also he is naturally invisible to the spiritual realm because he is uncreated and transcendent. The divine dimension is not the same as the spiritual dimension. God is not naturally visible even to angels. Thus even the appearance of God before the angels in heaven is a theophany.[9]

So, it would not be accurate to claim our sight of God in the new heaven and new earth will be of God's unveiled glory. We will see His face (Rev. 22:4), and yet, in His essence, He has no face. Nonetheless, that sight will be a sight the likes of which we have

---

9.   Cottrell, *God the Creator*, 231.

never seen during our time on this earth. It will truly be *awesome*, and it will supremely and perfectly satisfy us for all eternity.

Francis Chan, in his book *Letters to the Church* writes,

> You are going to see God soon. There's no way I can exaggerate how overwhelmed you will be. The most tragic mistake you can make on this earth is to underestimate how vulnerable you will feel when you see His face. And the wisest decisions you will make in life will be the ones you make with that final moment in mind.[10]

Similarly, Martyn Lloyd-Jones said, 'All I have tried to say can be put like this. You are going to see God! Do you not agree that this is the biggest, the most momentous, the most tremendous thing that you can ever be told? Is it your supreme object, desire and ambition to see God?'[11]

Stop for a moment, right now, and meditate on the gravity and the weight of that truth. You will see God. It will be more awesome and more humbling than anything we could imagine. Resist the urge to read on and simply finish this chapter. Hardly anything can do you more good than taking time to stop and face up to what it will be like when that moment arrives. Contemplate it and let it hit you.

How does looking forward to our reward change the way we are living and pursuing God now? Because, rest assured, it *will* change things. Sometimes it is said of Christians that they are so heavenly minded they are of no earthly good. In other words, they are simply withdrawing from the world and waiting to be taken out of it. I have actually found the opposite to be true. The more heavenly minded a person is, the more they love and risk for the good of others and the glory of God. The less they are troubled and stressed by current events. There is a peace and a confidence about them that is irresistibly attractive.

Doing what I have been describing in this book thus far is the best way to prepare for that moment when we will finally see the Lord face to face. Seeing God now prepares us for seeing Him after death. In fact, we could go so far as to say that seeing God now is a

---

10. Francis Chan, *Letters to the Church* (Colorado Springs: David C. Cook, 2018), Kindle loc. 2017.

11. D. Martyn Lloyd-Jones, *Studies in the Sermon on the Mount* (Grand Rapids: Eerdmans, 1976), 99.

prerequisite or requirement for seeing Him on that day. The puritan John Owen once wrote, 'No man shall ever behold the glory of Christ by sight in heaven who does not, in some measure, behold it by faith in this world.'[12] In other words, those who do not behold God with the eyes of their hearts by faith before death prove they have not been born again. They have not had their eyes opened. Therefore, they will not see God in eternal life. Their only sight of Him will be His condemnation on Judgment Day.

But for those who have been born again, we are like the blind man in Mark 8. When Jesus had spat on his eyes and put His hands on him, the man was partially healed of his blindness, but his vision was blurry. He could make out the forms of people walking around, but they looked like trees. In the same way, we see a dimmed or veiled form of God's glory now. But also, like the blind man, there will come a time when our eyes are further opened, and our sight becomes clear. As God spoke through the prophet Isaiah, 'The time is coming to gather all nations and tongues. And they shall come and see my glory' (Is. 66:18).

---

12.   Owen, *The Glory of Christ*, 4.

CHAPTER 17

GOD SEES US

A few years ago, I developed an unexpected relationship with a retired minister named Brad. God, in His wisdom and care, put him into my life during a time of deep frustration and confusion. For whatever reason, God put me into Brad's life during his battle with cancer that eventually led to his death. Brad had a fervent passion for mentoring and helping younger men in full-time ministry. He also had a unique ability to understand my emotions and frustrations at a time in life when it seemed like few others did.

I remember one afternoon at our church when Brad attended a lunch event for our retired folks. Brad hadn't been out to many public events in a while due to his cancer treatment, and everyone was excited and encouraged to see him back. As I walked into the room, Brad motioned for me to come over and talk with him for a bit. At one point, during the conversation, Brad leaned over, like he wanted to say something private, so I leaned in as well. I will never forget what he said. 'John, I know something about you.' I apprehensively replied, 'What's that?' He said, 'Everyone around here thinks you're a preacher. But I know better... you're a pastor.' I tried hard to conceal my surprise and emotion.

Now, for you to understand why that statement had such an impact on me, you need to understand my mindset in ministry at that time. I was confident I could preach, but I had all kinds of doubt and insecurity about my abilities in other areas of ministry, specifically pastoral care. Brad saw something in me that I didn't even see in myself.

A couple months later, I visited Brad in the hospital. His condition had deteriorated significantly. As I walked in and sat by his side, he woke up just long enough to ask me two questions, and then he fell back asleep for the rest of the time I was there. I'm so thankful God allowed him to wake up and speak because of what he said to me. At this point in my life, I was searching for a full-time preaching ministry at a church. I had no idea where God would lead me, but I knew without a doubt that he had called me to preach the Word. However, the job search had become extraordinarily frustrating. There were times when I felt angry, hopeless, depressed, apathetic, and sometimes a combination of them all. To make things worse, it felt like no one understood.

In that moment, in that hospital room, Brad woke up, and the first thing out of his mouth was, 'Have you heard anything about the job search?' He was dying of cancer and his first concern was my well-being. I said, 'No, still nothing.' Then he said, 'Are you discouraged?' I said, 'Yes.' Then Brad fell back asleep. That was our entire conversation, but that simple question, *'Are you discouraged?'* was such a balm to my soul because it felt like there was at least one person who understood. I felt *seen* in that moment.

In this final chapter, I want to break from examining our pursuit of seeing God, and instead focus on the fact that God sees us. At times, seeing God is a frustrating pursuit. It's not easy to see what no one has ever seen (John 1:18; 1 John 4:12; 1 Tim. 6:16), or to see something that is invisible (Heb. 11:27). But even though we struggle to see God, we must never forget that He sees us. This truth will carry us through the times when seeing God seems all but impossible.

God Sees Everything

One of the fundamental attributes that sets God apart from all others is that He is omniscient— He knows and sees all. You will find this doctrine scattered all over the pages of Scripture. For example, we read in Hebrews, 'And no creature is hidden from his sight, but all are naked and exposed to the eyes of him to whom we must give account' (Heb. 4:13). God says through the Prophet Jeremiah, 'Can a man hide himself in secret places so that I cannot see him? declares the Lord. Do I not fill heaven and earth? declares the Lord' (Jer. 23:24).

Most often, in the Bible, this doctrine is used to remind us that we cannot hide anything from God. At the final judgment we will give an account for every sin, and even every thought or intention of our hearts. The 'end of the matter' in the book of Ecclesiastes is that 'God will bring every deed into judgment, with every secret thing, whether good or evil' (Ecc. 12:14). Part of growing in holiness and in the knowledge of God is coming to understand that hiding from God is pointless. Yes, we might know this is true intellectually, but our actions reveal that there are times when this knowledge has not translated to our hearts. So often, after we have committed sin, we avoid God by avoiding time in prayer or Bible reading, or avoiding our church family. As we walk with the Lord and grow in our knowledge of Him, we slowly learn to run *to Him* after sin instead of away from Him.

But the doctrine that God sees everything is also an astounding comfort to the Christian. Only God sees the deepest and darkest corners of my heart—the parts I don't even share with those closest to me. He knows my greatest fears, embarrassments, and shames. God sees not only all the evil I have ever done, but all I have ever thought, and yet He still loves me! We hide those things because we are afraid that if people knew them, they would reject us. Yet, God knows them all, and does not reject us! His compassion is greater than we will ever comprehend. As J. I. Packer once wrote:

> There is, certainly, great cause for humility in the thought that he sees all the twisted things about me that my fellow humans do not see (and am I glad!), and that he sees more corruption in me than that which I see in myself (which, in all conscience, is enough). There is, however, equally great incentive to worship and love God in the thought that, for some unfathomable reason, he wants me as his friend, and desires to be my friend, and has given his Son to die for me in order to realize this purpose.[1]

---

1. Packer, *Knowing God*, 42.

He Takes Notice of Us

Perhaps even more perplexing and wonderful is the fact that God takes notice of us at all. When we consider the magnitude of the universe He has created, we begin to catch a glimpse at how insignificant and small we are. Consider for a moment that it would take 1.3 million earths to fill the volume of the sun. Next, consider that the sun is the center of but one solar system, in a galaxy full of thousands. Furthermore, our galaxy is but one of the millions (and perhaps billions!) of galaxies in the universe. Of that staggering expanse, I am one little person on one little planet, and I will only live for seventy or eighty years, if the Lord grants me that many.

In light of that, David's words in Psalm 8 carry a bit more weight: 'When I look at your heavens, the work of your fingers, the moon and the stars, which you have set in place, what is man that you are mindful of him, and the son of man that you care for him?' (Ps. 8:3-4). I am such an infinitesimally small crumb of God's creation, and yet He knows the number of hairs on my head (Matt. 10:30), the number of days I have left to live, and every thought that has ever passed through my mind! I try not to use the word *awesome* very often, but here it would be an understatement for God. Common sense tells us we should be overlooked and forgotten in a universe so vast, and yet the Bible tells us that God *sees* us.

It is not simply that He observes us, but He knows us intimately. He knows our secrets, our sins, our joys, and our struggles. What a comfort to know that in every trial and season of suffering, He sees it—He knows. Notice the insight God gave to Moses as he wrote for us the record of the Israelites suffering under Pharaoh:

> During those many days the king of Egypt died, and the people of Israel groaned because of their slavery and cried out for help. Their cry for rescue from slavery came up to God. And God heard their groaning, and God remembered his covenant with Abraham, with Isaac, and with Jacob. *God saw the people of Israel—and God knew.* (Ex. 2:23-25, emphasis added)

In Genesis 16 we read the story of Hagar, servant to Abram's wife Sarai. Even though God had promised offspring to Abram, he and Sarai struggled to trust in that promise, and to wait upon the Lord to bring it about. Since Sarai was barren, they took matters into their own hands. At Sarai's suggestion, Abram slept with Hagar and she conceived. Even though it was Sarai who originally suggested the plan, she unsurprisingly begins to look upon Hagar with contempt. When she begins to treat her harshly, Hagar runs away into the wilderness.

In the wilderness, God appears to Hagar and speaks to her. He tells her to return to Sarai and Abram and be submissive to them. He also tells her that like Abram, her descendants will also be more than can be numbered. And of the baby in her womb, God says, 'Behold, you are pregnant and shall bear a son. You shall call his name Ishmael, because the Lord has listened to your affliction' (Gen. 16:11). Hagar's response is a beautiful confession of faith: 'So she called the name of the Lord who spoke to her, "You are a God of seeing," for she said, "Truly here I have seen him who looks after me"' (Gen. 16:13).

The Hebrew name Hagar gives to God here is *El Roi*. Hebrew scholar Robert Alter notes that the most evident meaning of this name is 'God who sees me.'[2] Hagar is one of the most poignant examples in all of Scripture of someone who feels like no one sees or takes notice of her, and yet God does. So much so, that she gives God a unique name, *the God who sees me*. When it seems as though no one else sees you, always remember, *God sees you*. He saw Hagar, the lowly servant mistress that was used and discarded, and He sees you.

Jesus Saw the Ones No One Else Saw

It is not uncommon for teenagers to feel like no one notices them. Sometimes they will say, 'It feels like no one knows I even exist.' Perhaps you have experienced this feeling during times of grief or suffering. It feels as though you cannot share your pain with anyone, and when you do, their attempts at sympathy reveal they do not truly understand.

Yet seeing and sympathizing with those in pain was a hallmark of Jesus' ministry. Take, for example, His interactions with those who had leprosy. This was a group of people who were intentionally outcast and left alone because of the contagious nature of their disease. They had to announce their presence to anyone within a certain distance. What would it feel like if literally everyone you

---

2. Alter, *The Five Books of Moses*, 53.

encountered averted their eyes and turned away from you? But Jesus saw them. He looked at them, addressed them directly, and even touched them.

Recall Jesus' interaction with the woman caught in adultery in John chapter 8. The Pharisees saw only a lawbreaker—someone they could use to trap Jesus in His words. Yet Jesus saw her as a person, a woman, with emotions and a soul. He saw her sin, yes, but He also saw her need.

Consider His interaction with the woman who had been bleeding for twelve years (Matt. 9; Mark 5; Luke 8). He was on His way to heal Jairus' daughter, and it was urgent because the daughter was at the point of death. Yet He stopped and took time to address this woman, because He saw her. He saw her plight, her suffering, her frustration, and her desperation. To everyone else she was just a woman in a crowd. Not to Jesus.

Finally, consider the widow who gave two small copper coins as her offering (Mark 12; Luke 21). To those who were watching this was simply a woman giving a small sum. Some might have even wondered what was the point in giving such an insignificant amount of money. But Jesus saw her with spiritual eyes and said, 'Truly, I say to you, this poor widow has put in more than all those who are contributing to the offering box. For they all contributed out of their abundance, but she out of her poverty has put in everything she had, all she had to live on' (Mark 12:43-44).

To Be Seen Is Greater Than Seeing

Our great pursuit is to see the Lord, but being seen by Him is the greater privilege because of who He is. Think about what it would be like if the President of the United States knew you (for this illustration, imagine it was a President you greatly admired). There are many people who know who the President is, and what he does. There are some who speak to him and interact with him. But what if he considered you one of his closest friends? What if he came to you when he needed to vent or unwind? Think of how privileged and honored you would feel!

The Apostle Paul wrote of this in a few places in the New Testament. For example, in Galatians we read, 'But now that you have come to know God, *or rather to be known by God*, how can you turn back again to the weak and worthless elementary principles of the world, whose slaves you want to be once more?' (Gal. 4:9, emphasis added). In 1 Corinthians he writes, 'But if anyone loves God, he is known by God' (1 Cor. 8:3).

It is one of the great comforts of the Christian life to know that God sees and knows us. Specifically, it comforts us to know that He understands our sufferings and our weaknesses. In Psalm 1:6, David writes, 'for the Lord knows the way of the righteous, but the way of the wicked will perish.' In other words, through David, God is giving us words of encouragement, that even though at times it seems as if the wicked prosper and the righteous suffer, God sees us all, and He will ensure true justice prevails in the end. Your sacrifice to live in God's righteous ways will not go unnoticed. The arrogant rebellion of the wicked will also not go unnoticed.

One of the most comforting verses in the entire Bible for me is Psalm 103:14, 'For he knows our frame; he remembers that we are dust.' In other words, God is not surprised when we fall to moments of weakness. He understands that we are not perfect. He is gracious and compassionate, like the father teaching his child to learn how to walk. He does not chastise his baby girl after she takes one step and then falls. He picks her up and helps her to try again. As Jesus said to His disciples in the Garden of Gethsemane, 'The spirit indeed is willing, but the flesh is weak' (Matt. 26:41).

Seeing God is what this book has been all about. But it is no easy task, and often it seems impossible. In those moments let us remember that there is something more important than our ability to see Him. It is the knowledge that He sees us. In a book that is in many ways about seeing God, J. I. Packer writes, 'What matters supremely, therefore, is not, in the last analysis, the fact that I know God, but the larger fact which underlies it—the fact that *he knows me.*'[3]

---

3. Packer, *Knowing God*, 41. Your emphasis?

Conclusion

Seeing Him who is invisible

In the book *Unbroken*, Laura Hillenbrand tells the riveting story of Louie Zamperini, a World War 2 airman who faced overwhelming challenges and horrific conditions as a prisoner of war in Japan. It is one of the best books I have ever read and I would highly recommend it. Toward the end, after Zamperini has finally been freed and returned to America, we learn of his conversion to Christianity through hearing one of Billy Graham's sermons at the famous Los Angeles crusade of 1949. Zamperini was deeply convicted and unnerved when he heard Graham say the following: 'What God asks of men is faith. His invisibility is the truest test of that faith. To know who sees him, God makes himself unseen.'[1]

Those words of the great evangelist could hardly be more fitting as we come to the end of this book. Throughout this study, we have seen how God is a God who both hides Himself, and reveals Himself—and therein lies the key to seeing God. He hides Himself, in that He makes Himself invisible, unapproachable, and forbids us to visualize Him with images of our own making. But He also consistently takes the initiative to reveal Himself to us. After Adam and Eve forfeited their place in His presence, He made a way for

---

1. Quoted in Laura Hillenbrand, *Unbroken: A World War II Story of Survival, Resilience, and Redemption* (New York: Random House, 2014), 375.

Him to dwell in the midst of the Israelites through the tabernacle, and later the temple. He revealed Himself through the prophets and the words He gave them to speak to the people. He revealed Himself supremely through the incarnation of Jesus. He further reveals Himself through human beings created in His image, through creation, through moments of transcendence, and through suffering. And He has revealed Himself fully and definitively, once for all, through His revelation—His Word, the Bible.

We are seeking to do the impossible, to see Him who is unseen. This unseen God may be invisible, unapproachable, and unable to be visually represented in any way, but He has left us the means to see Him. This we *must do*, if we wish to spend eternity with Him in paradise. We must do what Moses did; we must see 'Him who is unseen' (Heb. 11:27, NASB).

We began this book with a look at Psalm 27, where we see that David's single-minded focus was on one thing: to dwell in the house of the Lord and to gaze upon His beauty (Ps. 27:4). Later, in that same psalm, David writes, 'You have said, "Seek my face." My heart says to you, "Your face, Lord, do I seek." Hide not your face from me. Turn not your servant away in anger, O you who have been my help. Cast me not off; forsake me not, O God of my salvation!' (Ps. 27:8-9). Another way to describe our pursuit to see God is that we are seeking God's face. When Moses asked to see God's glory, God told him he could see His back, but not His face, because no one can see that and still live (Ex. 33:18-20). Yet, at the same time, David tells us that God has said, 'Seek my face.' Impossible, but essential.

We find great encouragement, however, in God's many promises that if we seek Him with all our hearts, He will make sure that He is found. 'You will seek me and find me, when you seek me with all your heart' (Jer. 29:13). 'But from there you will seek the Lord your God and you will find him, if you search after him with all your heart and with all your soul' (Deut. 4:29).

> And you, Solomon my son, know the God of your father and serve him with a whole heart and with a willing mind, for the Lord searches all hearts and understands every plan and thought. *If you seek him, he will be found by you*, but if you forsake him, he will cast you off forever. (1 Chr. 28:9, emphasis added)

In his book, *Eyes Wide Open*, Steve DeWitt tells the beautiful story of how Hellen Keller came to faith in God:

> As a very young girl, Helen Keller contracted scarlet fever, which left her completely deaf and blind—essentially unable to communicate at all. At a young age she began asking the basic human questions: Where did I come from? Where will I go when I die? A twenty-year-old woman named Anne Sullivan became her teacher, and they developed a relationship that would continue for forty-nine years. The big breakthrough for communication came when Miss Sullivan made motions on Helen's palm while running water on her hand. Helen figured out that the motion symbolized the idea of water. From there she learned to speak by holding her fingers over another person's mouth as they spoke and mimicking the shape of their mouth to form words. She learned Braille and was able to read not only English but French, German, Greek, and Latin. Amazing. On one special day, Miss Sullivan decided to tell Helen about God. After the explanation, Helen responded that she already knew Him—she just didn't know His name.[2]

Can you imagine being Anne Sullivan, and doing your best to tell Hellen Keller about God, only to have her respond by saying she already knew Him, she just didn't know His name? It would make sense that those who lack the ability to see with their physical eyes would more easily learn to see with the eyes of their hearts. Believers like Helen Keller, or the famous blind hymn writer Fanny Crosby, are models to the rest of us.

For those who follow Jesus, we will spend the rest of our lives on this impossible but essential quest. To see God is our heart's great desire. One day we will be in His presence, our eyes will behold Him, but until then we will strive, with everything we have, to see Him by another means—the eyes of our hearts. For we know that it is true now, even as it will be true then: if we can behold His glory, it will change everything (2 Cor. 3:18).

---

2.   DeWitt, *Eyes Wide Open*, Kindle loc. 1029

Scripture Index

Genesis

Genesis 1:3 112
Genesis 1:26 46
Genesis 1:26-27 33
Genesis 1:27-28 46
Genesis 3:8 15
Genesis 4:26 78
Genesis 5:1-3....................... 46
Genesis 9:6 47
Genesis 12:7-8 77
Genesis 16:11 159
Genesis 16:13............. 22, 159
Genesis 18:1........................ 15
Genesis 28:16-17................ 72
Genesis 32:28...................... 20
Genesis 32:30...................... 21

Exodus

Exodus 2:23-25................ 158
Exodus 3:1 19
Exodus 3:5 76
Exodus 3:6 72
Exodus 3:14........................ 38
Exodus 19:16-20 72
Exodus 20:4 28
Exodus 20:18-19 72
Exodus 24:9-11 14
Exodus 32:4-5..................... 29
Exodus 33 36
Exodus 33:11................ 15, 21

Exodus 33:18................. 20, 59
Exodus 33:18-20 164
Exodus 33:20 ....20, 59, 152
Exodus 34:6-7..................... 59
Exodus 34:29-30................ 78

Leviticus

Leviticus 10:1-3................... 23

Numbers

Numbers 12:8 15
Numbers 25:7-9 50
Numbers 25:10-11.............. 50
Numbers 32:23 105

Deuteronomy

Deuteronomy 4:29 ... 128, 164
Deuteronomy 5:24-26 22
Deuteronomy 34:10............. 21

Joshua

Joshua 5:13-15..................... 76

Judges

Judges 2:1-3......................... 77
Judges 6:22–23..................... 22
Judges 13:22......................... 22

1 Samuel

1 Samuel 3:21 59

1 Samuel 13:14.............50, 122

1 Kings
1 Kings 18:21.....................106
1 Kings 22:19.......................16

2 Kings
2 Kings 17:15 80

1 Chronicles
1 Chronicles 16:11 129
1 Chronicles 28:9.......128, 164

2 Chronicles
2 Chronicles 18:18 16

Job
Job 19:21.............................21
Job 19:25-27.........................95
Job 23:12............................140
Job 40:4-5............................74
Job 42:5-6............................74

Psalms
Psalm 1:6 161
Psalm 8:3-4.......................158
Psalm 10:1 92
Psalm 11:7...........................104
Psalm 13:1-2 92
Psalm 17:3...........................109
Psalm 19:1-2 64
Psalm 19:9 107
Psalm 27:4 ....11, 127, 164
Psalm 27:8-9 164

Psalm 36:9 113
Psalm 37:4 .... 17, 128
Psalm 42:1-2 123
Psalm 51:6 105
Psalm 56:8 93
Psalm 63:1 123
Psalm 86:11........................107
Psalm 88:6-8.........................96
Psalm 103:14...................... 161
Psalm 115:8..........................80
Psalm 135:18.........................80
Psalm 139:13.........................47

Proverbs
Proverbs 1:7 73
Proverbs 9:10................ 73, 107
Proverbs 17:3........................95
Proverbs 20:9 109

Ecclesiastes
Ecclesiastes 3:11...................24
Ecclesiastes 12:14...............157

Isaiah
Isaiah 6:1-5 16
Isaiah 6:5 73
Isaiah 6:9-10 86
Isaiah 6:10...........................80
Isaiah 45:15..........................98
Isaiah 53:2 44
Isaiah 53:11........................126
Isaiah 55:6..........................128
Isaiah 66:2 108
Isaiah 66:18........................154

Jeremiah

Jeremiah 3:15 50

Jeremiah 23:24 157

Jeremiah 29:13 128,
138, 143, 164

Ezekiel

Ezekiel 16:42 85

Ezekiel 36:26 110

Ezekiel 48:35 119

Daniel

Daniel 7:15, 28 73

Amos

Amos 1:9 16

Matthew

Matthew 5:3 89

Matthew 5:8 103

Matthew 5:14-16 116

Matthew 5:20 105

Matthew 6:24 ....82, 106

Matthew 6:33 122

Matthew 7:7 128

Matthew 9 160

Matthew 10:30 158

Matthew 13:10-17 40

Matthew 13:13 82

Matthew 13:44 84

Matthew 15:18-19 106

Matthew 19:16-22 82

Matthew 26:41 161

Matthew 27:46 100

Mark

Mark 5 160

Mark 12 160

Mark 12:43-44 160

Mark 15:39 78

Luke

Luke 2:25-32 127

Luke 5:8 74

Luke 8 160

Luke 21 160

John

John 1:1 37

John 1:4-9 114

John 1:10-11 35

John 1:14 56

John 1:18 .... 13, 36, 104

John 1:29 41

John 2:19 56

John 3:3 .... 87, 133

John 3:5 87

John 3:14-15 132

John 3:19-20 32

John 3:19-21 .... 83, 115

John 3:30 75

John 4:24 ....28, 57

John 5:37 82

John 5:39-40 87

John 5:44 82

John 6:45-46 14

John 8:42 39

John 8:44 85

John 8:51-59 38

John 9:39-41 81
John 10:25-27 40
John 12:21............................ 44
John 12:35-36 115
John 12:41.............................58
John 12:45............................ 44
John 12:46............................115
John 14:6...............................39
John 14:6-7 36
John 14:9-10..........................37
John 20:28 39

Acts

Acts 2:38...............................48
Acts 4:13...............................79
Acts 4:18-20..........................80
Acts 5:40-41 96
Acts 7:54-60 151
Acts 9:4.................................74
Acts 9:15-16..........................94
Acts 12:21-23........................83
Acts 14:17 63
Acts 17:26-27.........................55
Acts 17:27 .... 17, 24, 64, 122

Romans

Romans 1:18 ....32, 65
Romans 1:18-21 64
Romans 1:18-21, and 10:14-17
                                      84
Romans 1:18ff..................... 40
Romans 1:19-21 24
Romans 1:20.........................14
Romans 1:23.........................29

Romans 2:14-15 24
Romans 2:28-29................... 40
Romans 3:21-26 42
Romans 5:3-4.........................97
Romans 6:17 110
Romans 8:18, 24 149
Romans 8:28..........................97
Romans 9:5............................39
Romans 10:17 ....58, 61
Romans 11:7-12 86
Romans 11:33 133

1 Corinthians

1 Corinthians 3:7 47
1 Corinthians 3:16-17 56
1 Corinthians 6:19 56
1 Corinthians 8:1 57
1 Corinthians 8:3...............161
1 Corinthians 9:27 143
1 Corinthians 10:21 104
1 Corinthians 12:7 49

2 Corinthians

2 Corinthians 3:18 ....11, 51,
                                75, 80, 165
2 Corinthians 4:4..................84
2 Corinthians 4:4-6 117
2 Corinthians 4:6..................87
2 Corinthians 5:7 149
2 Corinthians 9:7...............122
2 Corinthians 10:5...............99
2 Corinthians 11:14-15 55
2 Corinthians 12:9...............94

Galations

Galatians 2:16......................42

Galatians 4:9.....................161

Galatians 5:22-23 49

Ephesians

Ephesians 3:19 133

Ephesians 4:17-18 84

Ephesians 5:8-14................117

Ephesians 6:12...................118

Philippians

Philippians 2:5-7.................52

Philippians 2:15 117

Philippians 3:1, 4:4 122

Philippians 3:10 95

Philippians 3:21 44

Colossians

Colossians 1:15 .... 14, 36, 40

Colossians 1:19 and 2:9, ...39

Colossians 3:10 49

1 Thessalonians

1 Thessalonians 5:17...........125

2 Thessalonians

2 Thessalonians 2:10 84

2 Thessalonians 2:11-12........85

1 Timothy

1 Timothy 1:17....................14

1 Timothy 1:17, 6:16 152

1 Timothy 2:5 73

1 Timothy 6:9-10.................82

1 Timothy 6:16 .... 14, 23, 119, 156

2 Timothy

2 Timothy 2:7 ....141, 143

2 Timothy 3:16 92

2 Timothy 4:8 44

Titus

Titus 2:13 39

Hebrews

Hebrews 1:3 40

Hebrews 1:8........................39

Hebrews 2:10......................95

Hebrews 3:12-13..................88

Hebrews 3:13 84

Hebrews 4:14-16 74

Hebrews 10:4......................42

Hebrews 10:29 23

Hebrews 11:10 150

Hebrews 11:14...................150

Hebrews 11:27 .... 156, 164

Hebrews 12:2..................... 44

Hebrews 12:7,10-11..............97

Hebrews 12:14 ....88, 105

Hebrews 12:29.....................57

James

James 1:2-4 97

James 1:27..........................104

1 Peter

1 Peter 1:19 54

1 Peter 2:2.........................122

1 Peter 2:12 51

2 Peter

2 Peter 1:2...........................39

1 John

1 John 1:5............................57

1 John 2:8-10..................... 116

1 John 2:15...........................82

1 John 2:23 39

1 John 3:2 43

1 John 3:6..........................104

1 John 4:8, 16................ 16, 57

1 John 4:20 52

1 John 5:13.........................123

3 John

3 John 11...........................104

Revelation

Revelation 19:10...................76

Revelation 21:23-25, 22:5 ..118

Revelation 22:4 152

Also available from Christian Focus Publications...

The Person
of Christ

Finding Assurance by Walking With Jesus

Andrew Bonar

ISBN: 978-1-5271-0971-1

The Person of Christ:

Finding Assurance by Walking With Jesus

by Andrew Bonar (1810-1892)

Right views of sin have a tendency to lead us to right views of the Person of the Saviour. But the converse is also true; right views of the Saviour's person lead to the right views of Sin.

The Person of Christ is a wonderful encouragement for Christians today. Despite the difference between this edition's original publication date, the truths Bonar addresses are timeless.

Focusing his structure on topics from the person of Christ as the essence of good tidings to views on Christ and the second coming, Bonar sets out a precedent for heartfelt evangelical exposition of the Gospel via the personal relationship Christians have with the Person of Christ.

Christian Focus Publications

Our mission statement –

STAYING FAITHFUL

In dependence upon God we seek to impact the world through literature faithful to His infallible Word, the Bible. Our aim is to ensure that the Lord Jesus Christ is presented as the only hope to obtain forgiveness of sin, live a useful life and look forward to heaven with Him.

Our books are published in four imprints:

CHRISTIAN
FOCUS

Popular works including biographies, commentaries, basic doctrine and Christian living.

CHRISTIAN
HERITAGE

Books representing some of the best material from the rich heritage of the church.

MENTOR

Books written at a level suitable for Bible College and seminary students, pastors, and other serious readers. The imprint includes commentaries, doctrinal studies, examination of current issues and church history.

CF4•K

Children's books for quality Bible teaching and for all age groups: Sunday school curriculum, puzzle and activity books; personal and family devotional titles, biographies and inspirational stories – because you are never too young to know Jesus!

Christian Focus Publications Ltd,
Geanies House, Fearn, Ross-shire,
IV20 1TW, Scotland, United Kingdom.
www.christianfocus.com